THE MANY FACES OF ANXIETY
DOES ANXIETY HAVE A GRIP ON YOUR LIFE?

by
SUSAN RAU STOCKER

Holy Macro! Books

Box 82, Uniontown OH 44685, USA

The Many Faces of Anxiety
© 2013 Susan Stocker

Author: Susan Rau Stocker

Editor: Malvina T. Rau

Layout: Tyler Nash

Cover Design: Bob D'Amico & Shannon Mattiza

Published by: Holy Macro! Books, Box 82, Uniontown OH 44685, USA

Distributed by: Independent Publishers Group, Chicago, IL

First Printing: September 2012. Printed in USA

ISBN: 978-1-61547-016-7 (Print); 978-1-61547-207-9 (PDF); 978-1-61547-107-2 (Kindle); 978-1-61547-328-1 (ePub)

Library of Congress Control Number: 2013938512

Contents

INTRODUCTION

When we humans give a speech or pet a snake, most of us feel anxious. If we get pulled over by the police or draped with a paper bib in the dentist's office, we recognize the pounding heart and sweaty palms as anxiety. A first date, a job interview, our yearly review at work, reliably produce anxiety, as well. The Many Faces of Anxiety is not about these isolated but predictable life experiences.

When there is a *cause*, like a strange noise during the night, a stranded car on a dark road, or a trip to the emergency room, we expect anxiety. Since there is a *cause*, there is an *effect*: anxiety. Anxiety is the body's warning system: pay attention, be alert, get ready for trouble, it reminds us. Our eyes pop open, and we straighten our spines. We try to prepare ourselves for the whir of the drill or the humorless stare of the police officer. *Which things* cause us anxiety, and *how much* of it, depend on our personal likes and dislikes. But there are events and situations and in-laws and outlaws which create anxiety for each of us.

The anxiety we are talking about in this book has no specific observable cause. Oh, it might have had a cause, or some group of causes, in the past, but now the anxiety comes out of nowhere, it comes when and as it pleases, and it stays until it chooses to go.

Anxiety is the feeling we get in our chests, our throats, our heads, our shoulders, our backs, even our knees and toes, which tightens us. Our chests feel constricted, our throats swell shut, our heads feel as though all the neurons are firing randomly but at once. Our backs, necks, toes and knees are stiff, tingly, non-fluid and uneasy. We're on guard. But why? No toddler is standing on the edge of a cliff. We're not tied to the train track. We're not naked in front of the Chamber of Commerce. But we *feel* as anxious as if we were in one of these situations. We feel vulnerable, powerless, exposed and unprotected.

We feel that danger is imminent, but we can't pinpoint where it's coming from. We have a sense of impending doom, but there is nothing on the horizon or the radar screen to support it. We're shaking and shivering, sweating and swaying. We're out of balance, out of rhythm and out of sorts. But there is no apparent reason and no present cause for these feelings.

Anxiety is that out-of-whack, things aren't okay, sense of dread and upset that can make us feel certifiably crazy. Anxiety is a feeling inside us, and we try not to let it show on the outside because it's **nuts**. And it makes us feel **nuts**. It's inexplicable and unreasonable. It bears no correlation to how much we've slept or what we've eaten or where we are or whom we're with. For a client's own description of anxiety, see Olivia's case study in <u>The Many Faces of PTSD</u>.

And now, let me introduce you to anxiety the same way I learned about it: one case at a time. Meet Dora, my first and finest teacher.

DORA

Her Story

She found her way into the Victim Assistance Program office where I was an intern. At Victim Assistance we had a counselor for domestic violence and two additional counselors who worked with victims of other crimes. But since this woman was barely verbal, they didn't know to whom to assign her. No one could figure out who she was, what had happened to her, or what she wanted. So, they assigned her to me, who, at 40, was the new kid on the block.

I was totally unprepared for and unqualified for Dora. But, as it happens sometimes, clients are clearly so wounded and so fragile, that once you begin with them, if you even say hello to them, you have no choice but to continue and try to get yourself up to speed with their unconventional and unintentional on-the-job training. To send such a vulnerable client elsewhere is perceived by them as yet another rejection, another abandonment.

For me the hardest part of working with Dora was staying awake. I was a single mom raising three boys, working four part time jobs and completing a graduate degree.

Anytime I encountered silence, I immediately fell asleep. An hour with Dora was 50 minutes of silence interspersed with maybe 10 minutes of information that required a lot of filling in of the blanks.

Dora's story told itself haltingly and cryptically. Dora had an older brother who was married and the father of two children. Dora adored her niece and nephew and babysat whenever possible. God only knows how she did it. She herself still lived with her mother and father. She didn't work; she was *unable*. I would not have left my children with her.

Dora's mother was a mysterious creature who lived with Dora but played no part in her life, except that apparently she cooked. As far as I could tell no *meals* were ever eaten at Dora's house, but there was food available to be consumed, always in solitude.

Dora's father, on the other hand, was ever-present in Dora's life, and he played a continual and despicable role in her life drama. He introduced Dora to drugs, specifically heroin. He was her supplier. When she did what he wanted her to do, she was rewarded with a needle and a fix. When she didn't do what he wanted her to do, she was treated to the initial stages of withdrawal. Before long, she complied with his wishes.

His wishes, what he wanted her to do, became disgustingly apparent. He wanted her to have sex with whomever he brought home. If she was reluctant or expressed repulsion, she was given more drugs, perhaps some Xanax or some prescription pain-killers, something to numb her resistance. The sexual activity was entirely at the whim of the buyer. Whatever the buyer wanted, the buyer could have, including sodomy or sadomasochistic sex, and this could be photographed or videotaped, as the buyer wished, all if the price was right.

Dora had been taught by her father how to please these men. Her father was her first and most constant sexual predator. He taught her to be compliant, and he made sure she knew how to endure abuse. He made certain that she was "well-trained." Pain, punishment, and the withdrawal of that to which one is addicted, are powerful motivators.

Dora's father worked in a factory, so he had plenty of potential *friends* to bring around. What they paid depended on what they wanted. Dora received none of the money, of course. If she had the audacity to complain, her heroin supply dried up. By the time she was in eighth grade, she was dependably silent and reliably docile.

She acquired a new and additional perpetrator that eighth grade year. She walked out of her junior high school in the usual victim walk, head down, feet shuffling, and from under her lowered eyelids she couldn't help but notice a snazzy white limousine.

She realized that on various days different girls were invited to get into the backseat and when they accepted, the limo sped away.

One day she was chosen. She recalled feeling special. Finally, she was going to be the one selected. When asked if she'd like to "go for a ride," she silently nodded yes and slid in the open door. Off went the limo with a dreamy, happy Dora in the backseat.

She hadn't paid any attention to where they drove, she was just delighted to be riding in a limo. What eighth grade loser like Dora wouldn't be? Finally, the other girls would envy her.

The limo stopped at a park she didn't recognize. She could see out, but the windows were tinted so no one could see in. The limo driver crawled in the back seat with her and raped her. She was used to it. She wasn't even surprised. She was raped a couple nights a week, usually more than once a night. She didn't usually get a limo ride out of it.

Once it was clear to the limo driver that he'd get no resistance from this girl, he upped the ante. What he really liked was the feel of warm blood, and so he started cutting her vagina. Not all the time. Just some of the time.

Dora never knew if this would be the day she had a little ride, the day she got raped, the day she performed oral sex, or the day she got sliced and bled.

What this new uncertainty did was throw her even farther over the edge of sanity. Already she never knew which days her dad would bring a *friend* home, which days two or three *friends,* or which days the niece and nephew would appear and all would be familial and seemingly normal. But now the cutting in the back of the limo, with its added tension of when and how and how bad, resulted in debilitating anxiety. Dora's panic attacks and **episodes,** as her family called them, rendered her helpless, vulnerable, non-responsive in a corner, or hiding behind her clothes in her closet.

Then, with the resiliency of a trapped animal, she figured out how to calm her anxiety. If she cut her *own* vagina and made herself bleed, she could relax afterward. It was a brilliant, desperate solution. Whenever she caused her own traumatic event, which was a re-enactment of the trauma she endured from the limo driver, she could get herself to a different place in the anxiety cycle and experience the aftermath of relief.

The Cycle of Anxiety

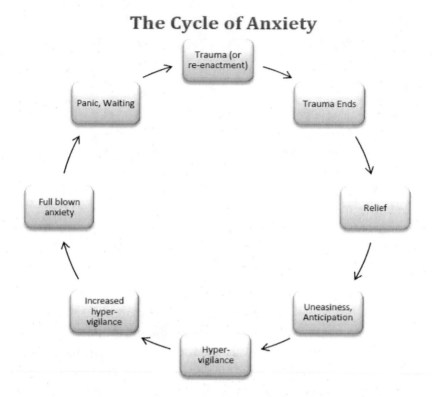

Here's the cycle in words: Trauma happens. After the trauma comes the relief that the trauma is over for now. And then the anxiety builds in preparation for the next onslaught of trauma. One starts scanning the radar for signs of the trauma approaching.

The scanning becomes hyper-vigilance. This state of hyper-vigilance, of constant red alert, becomes anxiety. The anxiety builds into panic. The panic and anxiety may ebb and flow from severe to moderate to mild, but the radar is always on, the tension always present, the waiting always taking its toll. And then, from out of somewhere, or out of nowhere, appears more trauma. And the cycle repeats. For Dora I would say the cycle repeated at least four times a week, 52 weeks a year, for about 20 years.

And so Dora became a cutter. She didn't cut her arms or legs or stomach, as do so many cutters. She cut her vagina and rectum. Over the time that I worked with her, she brought me six different pocket knives. I have them wrapped in a Native American scarf I was given at a women's retreat. I revere the pain they have caused and look at the wrapped knives to remind me of the pain I hope to help alleviate in large part because of what Dora taught me about anxiety.

After some time, Dora was able to understand what she was doing and she truly wanted to stop. But every time she gave me her weapon of self-destruction, she ended up getting another. The anxiety of *waiting* for abuse became more difficult and unbearable than the abuse itself. The waiting was worse than the abuse. This is puzzling until we factor in the relief. The relief can only come after the abuse. The abuse must be endured, and sometimes the abuse will be self-inflicted, to get to the only part of the cycle that doesn't contain anxiety. The relief.

◇◇

The relief can come only after the abuse.
The abuse must be endured to get the relief.
Sometimes, if the abuse is too intermittent,
The abuse will be self-inflicted.
Because the relief can come only after the abuse.

◇◇

After Dora and I had worked together for about a year, she drove past a middle school one day and saw the white limo. (Don't ask me how Dora could drive. I have no idea. Just as I wouldn't have allowed her watch my children, I wouldn't have permitted her to drive my car, either!) But she saw the white limo at a middle school and drove straight to Victim Assistance and flew, without announcement or appointment, into my office.

Even more amazing, she started talking. With some passion.

We called the detective bureau and asked for a detective to meet us at the Victim Assistance office to take Dora's statement. Dora was healthy enough not to want any other eighth grader to be chosen for a ride in that limo.

Dora made a lousy witness. She had just that once actually freely talked to me. Now here was a man, a stranger, a person of authority. Today I would have requested a woman detective for Dora. At that point I didn't have any of the nuances down. But, that day, together, we were able to get the story out and across to this police officer. "If nothing else," he promised Dora, "there will be no white limos loitering outside middle schools. That much I can promise. I'll try to do more, much more, but that, at least, I can guarantee." Unfortunately, he and I knew well (he, of course more clearly than I), that there were plenty of other forms of available transportation that might fill the bill for someone so demented.

Despite what she had done and what the police had promised to do, Dora slid into a deep depression from which I was never able to see her break free. Every Friday between one and two o'clock the phone would ring in the Victim Assistance office and those of us who were there would look at each other in sadness and resignation. We knew it was Dora.

"Is Susan there?"

"May I ask who's calling?" although we all knew her flat voice.

"Dora."

"I'm sorry, Susan's not here."

"Well, tell her I called to say good-bye." Slam. The phone went dead.

If I was there, I could expect an hour of my Friday afternoon spent fighting to stay awake as Dora and I baby-stepped through her suicide threats. Each week I would pray for some thought or phrase that might give her a reason to make it through more traumatic, abusive, anxiety-laden days and nights. What could anyone possibly say to Dora? She had no high school diploma, no work experience, at least none to be listed on a resume, and her great talent was enduring abuse.

If for some reason I couldn't be in the office on a Friday afternoon, one of the other counselors would try talking to Dora. We all gave it everything we had.

When I left Victim Assistance and went into private practice, Dora found me. She came to see me a number of times. Her actual abuse ended when her father retired and stopped bringing friends home from work. Dora found the strength to say, "No," to his advances, and unexpectedly, he put up no fight.

The heroin mercifully had tapered off gradually enough that it hadn't killed her. She was perhaps 40 at the time and looked 60. Her body and her spirit were so horribly wounded that it would be fair to say she was "broken."

One of the last things she ever asked me was if I still had the knives. I told her I did. She told me I should keep them. I reassured her that I would.

Her Signs

Dora was a *victim* through and through. Had you noticed her on the street, you would have turned away and tried to ignore her. Or you would have stared. She wore men's pants and shoes and old flannel shirts. Dora's hair color and length were so non-descript one would be hard pressed to be more specific than "dark." I have no idea what color eyes she had, nor could I really describe anything about her. She simply didn't stand out in any way.

◇◇◇

Female sexual abuse survivors frequently either dress like men or wear baggy asexual clothing, trying to camouflage any femininity in their bodies. Or, they may wear sexually revealing clothes which flaunt that for which they've been given attention. When I see someone dressed in an extreme way, sexual abuse survivor *always leaps to mind.*

◇◇◇

Dora *did not engage* others. She made *no eye contact* with anyone. Had you bumped into her on the street and said, "Oh, I'm sorry," she would have ignored you and hurried away. She *walked with her head down*, eyes fixed on her shoes. She shuffled, as though her feet were too heavy to lift. She carried no purse or bag of any sort and wore nothing of any color other than drab, if drab is a color.

Dora always came to see me at whatever time I suggested on whatever day I could see her. She had nowhere else to be. If I was late, she simply sat staring at her feet and waited. When I made the appointment for the next week and handed her the appointment card, she simply got up and left. She was *completely docile*. She never said "hello," and she never said "good-bye," except as a suicide threat. Dora and I never once exchanged a smile, nor did we ever share a laugh. To the best of my understanding, she had no acquaintance with humor. In fact, she was *humorless and lifeless*.

She *possessed no social graces*. I never heard her say "thank you," or "I'm sorry," or "please." If I offered her a cup of coffee or a cookie, she ignored me. She taught me to simply sit and wait. It was as hard for her to make herself talk as it would be for me to make myself throw up.

The picture of Dora that emerges, then, is one of someone who was *invisible*, wanted to be invisible, and preferred being invisible. Her anxiety was such that even being on the same sidewalk or sitting in the same waiting room with another human made her a nervous wreck. The only way she could tolerate proximity was to appear *indifferent and disengaged*.

Did Dora have other mental health diagnoses? Absolutely. She was, of course, a posttraumatic stress survivor, she suffered from depression, she was paranoid and she had schizoaffective disorder. And that's just what showed on the surface. Of the hundreds of people I have worked with in almost 25 years as a therapist, Dora was the most wounded and possessed the slimmest chance of any sort of recovery. She was the sickest person I ever have seen out in the world.

Unlike Carrie, the rape survivor in The Many Faces of PTSD, Dora had experienced nothing positive or normal before her trauma experiences began. She had no template of normalcy or sanity with which to contrast the insanity and abuse she endured. She may also have been quite limited in intelligence. For example, it never occurred to her to say "No," to the limo driver, or to exit the school from some other door. She possessed no beauty or grace or talents or skills, at least none that ever became obvious. More than anyone I've ever met, Dora needed loving, doting parents to build her self-esteem, help her experience love and joy, and equip her for her journey in this world.

Of all the burdens she carried, her anxiety was the most debilitating. Anxiety kept her body and mind in a constant state of hyper-alertness. Her ever-present *disguise* was her *lifeless apathy*. She, turtle-like, kept her head inside her shell. Like a chameleon, she tried to blend into the background and woodwork. Like a possum, she played dead. She was resigned to a painful, loveless, chaotic, meaningless existence.

Her Steps

Dora tried **individual therapy**. I believe I was the only therapist she ever talked to. I am not being falsely modest when I say that this is too bad for Dora. She needed someone with a great deal of experience and not someone brand new. But, she had no money and no way of knowing how to enter "the system." She wasn't a Medicaid recipient, had no insurance, and possessed no knowledge of what might be available to her. Unfortunately, she met me before I knew anything about helping someone navigate through the governmental mental health morass.

So, we worked together. I'm sure I was the first person who ever listened to her.

Dora came to **trust another human**, me, and I'm sure that was a first, too. However, it was a double-edged sword. The only reason she trusted me was because I never went behind her back, getting her admitted to the psychiatric ward for an assessment, for example, or pressing her to see a psychiatrist and start on medication. A more experienced therapist would have known how to get her into the system so she could get some medical assistance. I neither knew enough to try, nor did I believe she would do anything other than disappear if I pushed in any way. She was not about to give up her anonymity and invisibility.

Dora **allowed herself to be treated with respect**, which I'm sure was yet another first. Sometimes when I was particularly sleepy and she was particularly silent, I'd tell her stories. The stories were about anything that came to mind, my childhood, my kids, my worries. I have always imagined that she clung to some of these stories like lifelines, since she had none of her own normalcy on which to rely. I would talk about feeling depressed or anxious and describe what I did in this case or that. Sometimes I just made stuff up and tried to help her **learn coping skills**, albeit in story form.

I praised and validated every aspect of Dora that I could possible unearth. I reminded her how brave and tenacious she was to have endured so much and assured her that her very ability to survive was admirable. I would suggest things she might do to help her mom, in the hopes that this shadowy figure might notice Dora and reward her. I would talk about age appropriate games and activities for her niece and nephew, trying to make her a more popular aunt.

Dora **tried many suggestions** and was brutally blunt when reporting what didn't work. My ego took a beating, but that was the least of our concerns. I would ask her to write, draw, color, and she would. Her writing was illegible and difficult to translate into English. (She would always look at me as if I was a moron when there was a word I couldn't read. I took her idiosyncratic spelling as a personal challenge!) I have no idea how mentally impaired she was. Her social impairment was so severe and so complete that there were no channels available to pull out from her what intelligence may have been inside her. Dora had no communication skills, and the only way we ever know how bright or talented someone is comes from their *ability to communicate* their knowledge and wisdom.

◇◇

We know how smart someone is
*from their ability to communicate **their knowledge.***
Impaired communication and social skills
impair the perception of intelligence.

◇◇

Dora **showed up** for therapy. That was about all she would try. When I left Victim Assistance I suggested the community mental health services. I wrote down the information for her. She wouldn't take it from my hand. She refused to join a support group, refused to take any class or enroll in any sort of training. I saw her for free at Victim Assistance, of course, and "pro bono" where I was in private practice. I certainly didn't want her trying to earn any money doing anything she knew how to do so she could pay for therapy. So she came to see me. And then she stopped.

My Story

I really can't imagine what kind of therapist I'd be if I hadn't met Dora. The lessons she inadvertently taught me were so many and so varied, I should have paid her for her individualized instruction.

Dora taught me patience. Client's stories must be allowed to emerge. Therapists can't go in with blowtorches and hacksaws. Many times we are not going to get a chronological or an organized life chart. We are going to get disparate pieces and it's up to us to weave the threads into patterns and fashion the quilt.

Dora taught me invaluable lessons about social skills. She taught me, interestingly, how misleading and detouring–and sometimes downright devious–decent social skills can be. With Dora there were no tangents, no niceties, no sugar-coating.

I was not going to feel good at the end of a session with Dora. She was not going to tell me how much she'd learned in therapy or how helpful I'd been. I needed to regulate my own feelings and judge my own competency. For a million reasons this is a great therapist lesson: don't look for or depend on feedback from a client to make yourself feel good about what you're doing. Develop your own system of values and integrity. This is a kissing cousin of the idea I mentioned in The Many Faces of PTSD: no credit, no blame.

◇◇◇

Great and necessary therapist motto:
No Credit. No Blame.
Things go well in therapy: the client did it.
Things don't go well in therapy: the client did it.
No credit. No blame.

◇◇◇

Dora taught me the solace of "being with." She never, ever, said it helped for me to sit with her in silence or in listening. She simply kept coming back, for probably about two years. Nothing changed in her life during those two years. I was unable to help her help herself in any significant way. And yet she kept returning week after week. I came to understand that there is solace, a comfort, a balm, in having another as a witness.

◇◇

A witness provides solace.
A listener provides solace.
Seeing and hearing another's pain helps.
A listening witness gives solace to a wounded soul.

◇◇

Dora also taught me a lot about seeing through people's disguises. No make-up, no hair-style, no unconscious twirling of her hair or conscious slinging of her hair over her shoulders, no jewelry, no designer purse, no clean ironed clothes, no manners, no social skills, and yet there she was. A living, breathing person, body and soul. Absolutely complete and perfect in her incomplete imperfection. I doubt that I have ever looked at any person since Dora in the same way that I looked at people before Dora. We simply, assuredly, do not know what any person is enduring.

◇◇

People wear disguises and costumes.
Don't be taken in by them.
Don't be misled by the lack of them.
We are not the disguises we wear.

◇◇

Dora taught me to teach myself to stay awake. She taught me that I might never know the outcome. She taught me to honor the limits of the client. She taught me the patience of hearing the same thing over and over and saying the same thing over and over. (As I think about this aspect now, I realize it was like the necessity for repetition that my toddler granddaughter so appreciates. We learn by repetition. We just don't expect to encounter this need in adults.) She taught me not to push. She taught me to honor what I could not understand and to forego understanding for compassion.

Dora taught me once what Mother Theresa learned daily on the streets of Calcutta: The lesson of Namaste, which is a greeting used to acknowledge the divine spark in each other. Even the most unlikely, un-loveable, unapproachable, unfathomable person is a child of God holds a place in the family of mankind.

If I had another chance with Dora, I would change one thing for sure. If I could. I would hug her. Every time she came into my presence and every time she left, I would hug her. Here was a human who had never been touched non-violently and non-exploitatively. And I missed my chance to give her that free, invaluable, inalienably human gift of safe touch.

One last note to you who have just finished reading about Dora. I was at a book signing for The Many Faces of PTSD and a man picked up the book and took it over to the cafe in the bookstore and looked at it for about 45 minutes. Then he brought it back and handed it to me saying, "I can't read about these things." I just nodded, but what I was thinking was, "*Someone* had to live these things, and you, sitting in a nice, warm, safe bookstore can't *read* about them! The least we can do is read about them."

I know it is not easy to read about one person's inhumanity to another person, and that, of course, is the basis of posttraumatic stress, anxiety and depression. But until we see and admit and acknowledge and understand these things, we will miss them when they are in our midst. I have heard too many survivors ask me, "Do you think my mother knew?" Oh, yes. I think she knew. But she didn't want to see or admit or acknowledge, and she didn't understand the harm her silence and ignorance were perpetrating.

These stories are hard to read. But someone has lived each of them. Perhaps our reading about these difficult things will open our eyes and put courage in our hearts that we, at least, will not stand by silently and pretend we haven't noticed a thing. This makes me think about Joe Paterno, the Penn State football icon and the winningest coach in college football history. I wonder what he wishes he had done differently.

BRAD

His Story

Brad was the only child of older parents. His mother never worked and his father was a blue-collar worker who never played. His house was quiet and sterile. He was a lonely, silent, invisible child, the kind who never made a mess and never laughed. He had no temper tantrums, no giggles, no melt-downs and no misbehavior. Brad was perfect.

He was invisible at home and invisible at school. His third grade teacher said she would not have known Bradley's voice. He never spoke. But he made no trouble, and so no one wasted energy on him.

He got straight A's and seemed capable of solving any math or science problem that crossed his desk. He could write a grammatically correct paper with no misspelled words.

Brad ate lunch alone and was never seen on the playground. But since he caused no problems and knew how to stay under the radar, he was left to his solitary ways. And the kids never bothered him because he ignored their taunts. They couldn't get his goat, and that was no fun.

He was a short, chubby kid who rarely made eye contact and even more rarely combed his hair. He never missed school, but no one would have been able to attest to that, since people rarely noticed Brad.

He would have surprised everyone, had they been paying attention, by graduating from high school and getting a free ride to M.I.T. Brad left home that September on the bus, and he never returned. He wasn't mad at his parents, and they weren't mad at him. Years later, he returned for, first, his father's funeral and then his mother's. He called an auctioneer and a real estate agent, and when they had completed their jobs, he put his entire legacy into a savings account.

He married soon after, the first girl who had ever noticed him, and the unconsummated marriage lasted about nine months. She left with no animosity, just amazement, and Bradley returned to his familiar state of emotional hibernation.

Brad earned degree after degree in engineering and was sought after for government jobs. He designed things he could never talk about, but since he never talked anyhow, that was fine by him.

Through his 30s and 40s he worked and bought a house and operated ham radios and played a monthly poker game with college acquaintances and became an even stranger, more idiosyncratic fellow. He was brilliant and baffling. But he was also lonely and loveless.

Enter Barb. Brad and Barb met through an on-line dating service. They were the only ones to respond to each other's profiles. They fell in love.

She was an extrovert who was never quiet. If she stopped talking, she might cease to exist. She was creative, compassionate, nurturing, emotional and, in her mid-forties, childless. She had a chronic health condition which left her in constant pain and unable to work. She saw in Brad a needy, unloved little boy and assumed that silent waters run deep and that his paid-for-house and fabulous job would provide her with the stability she was lacking. He saw in Barb a friend who could interface for him and handle the business of life while keeping him company and keeping his house. He had no family. She had an exuberant, extravagant, inclusive Italian family quite accustomed to taking in strays. No one noticed that he didn't talk. They didn't know many brilliant engineers. Maybe he was just one of that group.

But an interesting thing happened to Brad when he entered the realm of Barb and her welcoming family. He developed an anxiety disorder.

As long as Brad didn't have to interact with anyone or compromise or negotiate or communicate, he wasn't anxious in the least. But put him in a family way, with a wife who had wishes and wants and a family who had holidays and birthdays and picnics and communions and parties . . . . trouble.

His Signs

Bradley did anxiety with the *obsessive/compulsive, exact perfectionism with which* he did everything else. Anxiety pervaded every aspect of his life.

Brad became a *hoarder*. He bought every motor and antenna and wiring system he could find. He bought hundreds of pallets. He bought every tool known to man, even though none of them were known to him. He then had to have a huge storage shed built to house all his acquisitions.

Barb got huffy about all the money Brad was spending on useless stuff, and so she started shopping. She came home one afternoon with $5,000 worth of new living room furniture. Their old living room furniture was stuff Brad had used since he was 22. That was irrelevant to him.

So was his spending of much more money than Barb on less visible and less useable things.

Brad took Barb off his checking account and cancelled her credit cards. Now he was not only hoarding stuff, he started *hoarding money* as well. Brad became a Scrooge of the first order. He was a cheap-skate. He was so tight he squeaked.

As his anxiety around *having everything he could ever possibly need in case of any possible, or impossible, catastrophic event* built, he financed these many contingencies by saving every possible penny and dime and dollar. Never mind that the house and both cars were paid off. Never mind that they had no credit card balances, and the savings account and the money market and the stock market were flush, flush, flush. Anxiety is not reasonable, logical or rational.

<><><><><><><><><><><><><><><><><><><><><><><><><><><><><><><><><><><><><><>

ANXIETY is not
reasonable,
logical, or
rational.

<><><><><><><><><><><><><><><><><><><><><><><><><><><><><><><><><><><><><><>

Brad started *obsessing* about the next domino in the stack to go. He was going to lose his job. If the boss called another engineer into his office, it could only mean that he, the other engineer, would be given Brad's projects and he, Brad, would be let go. The government was going to reject his designs. The company was going bankrupt. Hadn't they just closed their company cafeteria? What more proof could one want?

Oh, and the stock market, too, was going to crash. Never mind the fact that one day when the stock market itself took a dive, Brad, in his idiosyncratic wisdom, made over $100,000. In one day. Anxiety is not reasonable or logical or rational.

<><><><><><><><><><><><><><><><><><><><><><><><><><><><><><><><><><><><><><>

Remember: ANXIETY is not:
reasonable,
logical, or
rational.

<><><><><><><><><><><><><><><><><><><><><><><><><><><><><><><><><><><><><><>

The sky is falling, Chicken Little. And all Barb could do during this traumatic and trying time was buy more paint and bring home more stray puppies. She even went on the Internet and bought $3 rosaries for her sisters and Brad's dying aunt in West Virginia. That was the last straw. (I'm not sure who cried, "UNCLE.") Into therapy they came.

His Steps

So, the engineer who saves and the wife who spends come to **therapy** to talk about the marriage they both want to keep. It's months before the therapist learns that this four-year marriage, like Brad's first, is unconsummated.

Barb is depressed. This is not the bargain she entered into. Brad is anxious. This is not the bargain he entered into. She thought she had a wild-haired knight on a white (paid for) horse who would adore and protect her. He thought he had a helpmate who would keep the house in the sterile standard his mother had set and spend as little money as his mother had, all the while adoring him and interfacing with life for him.

Soon they are each on **anti-depressants and sleeping medications**. It turns out that neither takes the medication consistently or as prescribed. People with Brad's control issues have trouble giving in to medicine. People with Barb's diet of pain medication have trouble remembering to take their other medications.

I **see them separately**. Brad complains about Barb, and Barb complains about Brad. I reframe. I refocus. I tell them each what wounded children they have married. I explain that they have each entered into this union to be saved. I'm wasting my breath.

I **give them homework**. We work out a budget. To quell his anxiety, he needs some serenity about money. It's the only way to stave off his anxiety. To quell her depression, she needs some power to have some money to spend. It's the only way to stave off her depression.

Ostensibly, they both agree. Actually, he nitpicks and reneges and rescinds wherever possible. She, in return, starts becoming devious by taking cash from his wallet.

I beg her to start cooking, figuring that his being nourished in some way will ease things. She complies probably once a month. I beg him to take her on a vacation. They've managed that once in four years for three days by car to a neighboring state. They each report they laughed and had fun.

Years go by and Brad doesn't lose his job. The stock market goes way down, but, savvy fellow that he is, his portfolio grows. He becomes

somewhat more consistent in giving her a steady allowance, but, despite his financial successes, Barb's allowance stays meager.

He's stingy, she complains. It's his anxiety, I explain. His anxiety demands that he have savings in excess. Well, she moans, my anxiety demands I have money for gas and groceries and haircuts. Her requests seem reasonable. His anxiety and stinginess and withholding seem unreasonable and unkind.

Barb brings home stray animals who pee and poop on the floor. She hires workmen to do projects around the house that seem necessary to her, like keeping the grass mowed. Then, she expects Brad to pay them. She orders presents for ill and hurting people. She leaves him to pay the bills for that, too. And, to top it off, she won't go to bed with him at nine o'clock, and, so, he can't sleep because the house is not on lock-down.

If you want to be in control of your life . . . .
do not
take a wife.

My Story

Brad's anxiety is fueled by fear. Money equals security to him, and the lack of money equals vulnerability. When Brad can control his money, his environment, his schedule, his diet, Brad can relax and his fear dissipates and his anxiety recedes. When things are as sterile and predictable as they were when he was a child, his anxiety decreases. But, unfortunately for Brad, he also gets more depressed. He didn't thrive in his childhood. His childhood was predictable, though. Be depressed or be anxious? What a horrible choice.

Brad wants Barb and her family and the pets and the liveliness she brings. But these things incites fear because it is not a model home and she is not a model wife. He needs her to breathe life into him. But life and liveliness and joy all equate with uncertainty. The price to be paid for spontaneity and humor and fun is unpredictability.

Certainty is predictable stagnation.
Stagnation is death.
Uncertainty is unpredictable movement.
Uncertainty is life.

◇◇

Working with Brad and Barb is fascinating. They speak different languages. He speaks an evidence-based language, and she speaks an emotion-based language. He wants facts to quiet his fears. He wants rationality from Barb who speaks only emotion. She wants emotion from Brad who speaks only evidence. But sometimes, she tells me, in the dark of the night, he'll reach over and hold her hand.

Brad is a helpful study in anxiety for a number of reasons.

First of all, his childhood taught him fear. The sterility, the predictability, the lack of connection and bonding, the emotional vacuum, produced in Brad an emotionally stunted, terrified child who grew into a man intellectually and physically but remained an infant emotionally and spiritually. Brad grew up never having taken a tumble, and, therefore, Brad grew up not knowing that he could get up if he fell down. Brad grew up without resiliency.

Secondly, when Brad was alone, Brad experienced very little anxiety because he recreated in his adulthood the sterility, the predictability and the emotional isolation of his childhood. And, as in his childhood, it didn't feel good. It wasn't satisfying. But, it was familiar.

◇◇

A sterile environment is one in which nothing lives.
A sterile environment contains no plants and no pets.
Plants and pets make messes.
In a sterile environment everything has a place.
Everything knows its place, and everything stays in its place.
A sterile environment is essential for an operating room.
A sterile environment is deadly for a home.
What keeps people alive during surgery
Sucks the life out of them on a daily basis.

◇◇

Third, once Barb triggered Brad's anxiety, it ran amok. His anxiety leapt from fear of pee and poop from the pets–okay, so maybe he was potty-trained too early–to fear of financial ruin, to fear of loss of employment, to fear of the world economic structure collapsing, to fear of . . . poverty. The irony was that Brad's very fear kept him in emotional and spiritual poverty.

Fourth, anxiety leads to OCD (obsessive compulsive disorder), rage, irrationality, sleeplessness, stinginess, meanness, depression, apathy, condescension, frustration, intolerance, humorlessness, lack of generosity, perfectionism or dishevelment in personal style, oppositional and defiant behavior, and deep and unapproachable fear.

Fifth, Brad's fear-based anxiety was contagious.

◇◇

FEAR
is the most contagious emotion.
FEAR
is toxic.

◇◇

The fearful attitude Brad conveyed at work kept his colleagues away from him. The fearful attitude Brad conveyed at home had his wife in bed under the covers until he came to bed, at which point she leapt out of bed wide awake and was unable to sleep until morning when Brad left for work. His fear was too much for her. She had to avoid him to avoid his fear, which would have enveloped her and rendered her immobile.

In therapy the fear came out differently. Every single time he came into therapy – perhaps eight times in all – he announced uncompromisingly and definitively that this was his last time in therapy. Brad was scared to death of change. Therapy advocated change.

◇◇

Change is life.
Stagnation is death.

◇◇

As I write this, I see Brad's wife every week and Brad every three or four months.

We are simply keeping her depression from dropping too low and his anxiety from rising too high. This is not my most successful therapeutic involvement. But, as I mention frequently, it is all a process. Therapy is not a destination any more than life is. And, as Mother Theresa mentioned frequently, "Plant the seeds." You may believe that they can't grow, and perhaps they won't grow, or you may never know that they do grow. Plant them anyhow.

P.S. I have a client who is a guerrilla gardener. Have you heard of them? They carry seeds with them, I think usually sunflower seeds, and they plant them anonymously and secretly in unlikely places, thereby giving the world more lovely, sunny things. How unpredictably delightful is that?

P.P.S. I once told Barb that she seemed as fragile and as beautiful as an orchid. She looked at me in shock and asked me how I knew. How I knew what, I questioned? She loves orchids, she told me. She grows them. She has about 50.

◇◇◇

Believe in the metaphors.
Believe in what you can't prove.
Believe in what you do not and cannot know.
Believe anyhow.

◇◇◇

MIKE

His Story

Mike came into therapy with his wife and, as sometimes happens, they had rather different stories to tell. Let's start with his wife's story.

The economy is bad, was where Ann started. So, she lost one job, had a car repossessed, and lost another job. All of which amounted to her being home all day, stuck there with no transportation, and all she had for entertainment were the television and the computer.

So, Ann logged onto Facebook or Classmates or some such find-your-old-friends-and-lost-loves kind of place and, sure enough, she found some old friends. One of them offered to lend her some DVDs and so every couple days she would take Mike to work and go see the old friend and get some different DVDs.

Mike was unreasonably suspicious and paranoid. He had started a whole lot of checking behaviors which Ann found controlling and frustrating. She was just bored and this old friend was just lending her movies.

I dutifully tuned in to Mike's anxiety. What was going on? He was college educated and had a good job making more money than I did. He liked his work. He loved his wife. She handled the finances, and they had had a couple cars repossessed in the last years, they rented their home, and he couldn't figure out why they didn't have enough money.

Ann quickly added to the story, with some bitterness, that she had come into the marriage with some assets and they were all gone now. She sounded angry, and she spoke loudly. She was firm and certain of her reality, and Mike was overwrought and driving her crazy with his unfounded suspicions. She thought he was obsessive.

Mike went to the doctor and got on an anti-depressant with an anti-anxiety component. His wife reported that the "checking" behaviors slowed down. But they didn't stop. She had just about had it with him. He was making her life miserable. He would toss and turn all night, and she would find him on the computer in the wee hours looking up her history of use. It was invasive and crazy.

One day his wife was ill and instead of cancelling the appointment, he came by himself. As Paul Harvey would say . . . and now, the rest of the story.

21

Mike read Ann's e-mails. He read all of them, and there were many. He said demurely, "They were sexual in nature." Ann talked to this old friend on the computer and on the phone many times every day. Ann sent him pictures of herself in her underwear and in "various states of undress." Mike finally called her on the carpet when his snooping revealed that the last time she had gone to collect DVDs, the old friend had "whipped his monkey" for her. (I'd never heard that expression, but it is sort of a self-explanatory description.)

I said, appalled, to Mike: "You mean to tell me I have sent you to a doctor to get anti-depressant and anti-anxiety medication so you can tolerate a cheating wife?" Not likely to be on anyone's top 10 of brilliant therapeutic interventions.

They came back in together and I asked Mike to explain to Ann why he was so intent on checking. He told her he had found out about the sexual pictures and about the man masturbating in front of her. She told him to not get caught up in the details and to just get over it like she had.

She remained convinced, and convincing, that Mike's anxiety was the cause of their problems. I spoke up with a second opinion. I thought his anxiety was the result of their problems and a result of his inability to confront her openly and honestly.

His Signs

Mike's anxiety *kept him up at night* long after Ann had gone to bed. He was *checking her phone calls and her computer history* and then, after checking, he would stew about what he had found and what he might have missed.

He'd slip into bed in the early hours of the next day only to awaken thrashing and sweat-drenched. His first marriage had ended when his wife had had an affair. He had always wondered whether he should have stayed and tried to save his marriage. He had sworn to himself that this time he would be true to his vows and preserve his marriage no matter what. Now his second wife was having an affair right under his nose, lying about it, and telling him his anxiety was excessive and unfounded. He was on the horns of a dilemma: put up with a lying, cheating wife and be true to his vows, or, be true to himself and break his vows. Can't win with a dilemma like that.

His *concentration at work suffered* since, instead of doing his job with focus, it frequently occurred to him to call Ann or text her or see if she was on the computer. She was looking for a job, she argued, and she needed the computer and the phone to do that. Every time he found her on the computer or the phone he assumed it was with the monkey-handler.

As it so often does, Mike's anxiety slid him right into *obsessive thinking and compulsive behavior.* He couldn't stop ruminating about what Ann was doing and he couldn't stop checking up on her. He had to know. Except that when he checked and found something, he obsessed about that, and when he checked and found nothing, he compulsively kept checking.

Another common result of anxiety happened in Mike's case. He *stopped trusting.* He stopped trusting his wife, but he also stopped trusting himself and everyone else. Perhaps most devastating is the way we stop trusting our own intuitions, instincts, eyes and ears.

◇◇

A common result of anxiety is that we stop trusting.
We stop trusting others.
More of a problem is that we stop trusting ourselves.
We stop trusting our senses–what we see and hear.
We stop trusting our own intuitions.
We turn on others and we turn on ourselves.
Our basis in reality is shattered.
We lose our footing and our grounding.
We lose our self-trust and self-confidence.

◇◇

Because anxiety keeps us in a *state of hyper-alertness*, we set ourselves up for perceptual errors. Everything becomes something of significance. There is no small stuff anymore. There are no blips on the screen. (There are no birds in the sky; everything approaching us is an incoming missile–and it's seeking us on a search and destroy mission.)

Everything must be analyzed and assessed. A wrong number is "him" calling. Wrong numbers no longer exist except as an excuse. A car turning around in the driveway is "him" stopping by to see Ann, but turning and driving off when he spots Mike's car. Everything becomes part of the nasty puzzle. We see what we expect to see. We see what we dread seeing. We see our worst fears come true.

◇◇

Our anxiety alters our perceptions.
We make the "facts" fit the story we fear the most.
The story we fear the most causes and increases our anx-
iety.
Our anxiety alters our perceptions.

◇◇

Mike was blind-sided. While he was at work, he was trusting Ann to be at home doing what she said she was doing. Instead, she first did different things than she said she was doing, then she lied about doing different things, then she blamed her behavior on his reactions to her doing different things and lying about them, and then she told him to get over it.

Her cool logic and dismissive attitude kept him off balance. Maybe, he thought, she was telling the truth. Maybe it was nothing. Maybe he was just making mountains out of molehills. She said one thing, and he saw another thing in the computer records and phone logs. Do women send old friends pictures of themselves in negligees?

His Steps

Mike and I did a lot of **perception checking**. He is a very bright man, but he is the child of a critical mother who schooled him to believe that what he saw wasn't true and what he experienced wasn't reality. His passive, peace-at-any-price father didn't challenge his mom's skewed perceptions or stand up to her illogical conclusions. Mike himself was passive, naive, and much too willing to buy the swamp land in Florida. So, as often as possible, he just ran things by me and I gave him my rendition of "normal." No, Mike, married people do not send pictures of themselves in "various states of undress" to others. No, Mike, husbands should not need to check on their wives' computer histories to be able to go to sleep at night. And no, Mike, people who borrow movies from old friends do not usually get a titillating sideshow along with the movie. Usually, there is no monkey-business.

Ann remains unrepentant and unaccountable; therefore, Mike remains confused and anxious. What we have decided, Mike and I, is a two-pronged approach: #1, **wait and see**; and #2, **gather information.**

Mike's twin daughters, whose own mother was a sex addict, are about to start their senior years in high school. He'll wait and see, rather than uproot them again. He'll gather information. While Ann offers no nurturing to the girls, he and Ann do provide some stability. He doesn't want the girls to suffer unduly from his second unfortunate choice of mate.

◇◇◇

It's all just information.
Gather information.
Withhold judgment.
Draw no conclusions.
Just keep gathering information.
It's all just information.

◇◇◇

Pay attention. Gather information. Follow the process and the conclusion will become clear.

And, of course, there is the ever-present and always helpful Serenity Prayer: control what you can, let go of what you can't control, and learn to know the difference.

◇◇◇

God grant me the serenity
to accept the things I cannot change,
the courage to change those things I can,
and the wisdom to know the difference.

◇◇◇

My Story

Now, you've got to be confused, because in the introduction I stated unequivocally that the anxiety we were talking about in this book was not anxiety related to a situation which would cause anxiety in most of us: a cheating spouse. If Mike were not genetically and experientially predisposed to anxiety, he would react to a cheating, unrepentant, unaccountable wife with some range of anger, vengeance, disgust, a slammed door or divorce papers.

Neither Mike nor Ann, but especially Ann, was willing to allow me to delve into their pasts and look for patterns and explanations. More than any other couple I've ever worked with, they were interested only in the present problems and, from Ann's perspective, how to make sense of the disparity between what she said and what Mike discovered. Believe her explanations, was Ann's logical conclusion.

So, I've been stuck in this case, working from the present to the present. It's hard to go where a client won't follow. I can't explore their pasts without their cooperation. Mike, in the brief amounts of time I've been able to see him alone, is open and has told me about his critical mother and his passive father. When Ann is present, both of them resort to glossing over things.

I know absolutely that Mike's anxiety precedes this one situation. As adults we don't act or react out of character.

◇◇◇

As adults
we don't act
and we don't react
out of character.

◇◇◇

Had Mike not been prone to and experienced anxiety as a child and young adult, this situation would not have provoked an anxiety response.

If as kids we got angry or hurt or oppositional or depressed or anxious . . .

as adults we are likely to react on that same continuum.

When I see a client who presents as "anxious," it is helpful for us to backtrack. What started this anxiety in the first place? When do you first remember feeling anxious?

Oh, I hear, I was four, or I was in second grade. Typically the first memory of the response is very early. This helps us to figure out just what the anxiety is about and where we might begin to work to reduce and neutralize it.

I expect that Mike and Ann will divorce. As these things go, I would have to guess that Ann will leave Mike before he has a chance to leave her.

Ann is the more wounded of the two people here. She is the least approachable, the least honest, with herself as much as with Mike or me, and the least able to bond. I don't know, and almost certainly never will know, what has hurt her at such a deep level.

She will be unlikely to ever seek help.

Mike is likely to remain in therapy for self-esteem work and for some delving into his past. Mike has intimacy problems. In his first marriage there was a lot of sexualizing of love: swapping, three-somes, talk of having an open marriage and a great deal of sexual experimentation. All of this points to an inability to bond and a difficulty with intimacy.

Ann, too, has intimacy problems. Neither she nor Mike seems comfortable nor capable of monogamy. To me this indicates a lack of trust, a lack of nurturance from parents, and a multitude of unresolved issues from their childhoods. In other words . . . anxiety.

KATIE

Her Story

She was in eighth grade when I met her. She was chubby, wore braces and had purple hair. She had enormous blue eyes that should have been smiling and full of mischief. At that first meeting, they looked pretty haunted and filled with some mixture of anger, fear, defensiveness, and, perhaps, shame. Her parents had just discovered that she was slicing her arms with a razor. Katie was a "cutter."

Katie had two older brothers, a mom, a dad, and two cats living in her house. At the first run-through of her story, her family sounded like the Waltons. Dad taught in the middle school she attended, and mom stayed home, catered to the kids, and gave generously of her time and talents to the synagogue. Katie adored her brothers: the older was a yuppie-type high school tennis star, and the middle one, a self-contained musician.

Katie was a tomboy who loved to write. Both mom's and dad's families lived close, and she had lots of extended family visits.

We didn't talk about cutting that first time. There was enough defensiveness in her eyes that it seemed wise to spend some time bonding, find some common ground, and build some trust.

Katie was easy to like and talked like a magpie. Her boyfriend had dumped her for one of her close girlfriends. The other three close pals all sided with Katie and all four were united in their dislike of Heather, the boyfriend thief.

Katie told me a lot about these three close friends. What she omitted in the beginning was that all four of them were "cutters." They each worried incessantly about what the other three were doing, knowing full well that "cutting" was not the best answer to any question. They each staunchly maintained, though, why they themselves *had to cut.*

◇◇◇

Each client is a big jigsaw puzzle with thousands of pieces.
The client hands the therapist the pieces a few at a time.
Together you and the client examine the pieces.
You're putting together a complex and unique puzzle.

◇◇◇

Katie's mom suffered from anxiety and had from childhood. Add to that, she had been diagnosed with breast cancer when Katie was in fifth grade. She told Katie she did not want to die until all her children were raised. The musician son who was a junior in high school was purportedly mom's favorite. Katie wondered if mom would die when he was "raised," and she wondered what constituted "raising." Would that be high school graduation, college graduation, marriage, children of his own? What did it mean, and when would her mom stop fighting and die?

Katie's dad was a Vietnam combat vet who suffered from anxiety, depression and posttraumatic stress. She knew he had won all kinds of awards. She also knew he refused to talk about it. Katie's mom had told her that he had been forced to kill people in Vietnam and that because of it he was a shell of a man now. He wouldn't go to synagogue with them. He no longer believed in God. He believed in being the best teacher he could be and punishing himself with multiple-hour workouts at the gym every day after school. He'd go home, change his clothes, and go to his second job, which was selling insurance for the family business. Except for his job at the middle school his children attended, his kids rarely saw him and barely knew him.

◇◇◇

Both Katie's mom and dad suffered from anxiety.
Anxiety is frequently a family affair.

◇◇◇

When Katie and her brothers went to events on dad's side of th family, mom stayed home and "rested." When they went to events on mom's side of the family, dad was too busy to go along, even on holidays.

There were four bedrooms in their house and they were interestingly assigned. Mom had the master bedroom to herself. The brothers shared a room. Katie had a room. The fourth bedroom was dad's office. He spent his nights on the couch in that room.

◇◇◇

Where people sleep in a home is important information.
With whom they sleep is telling information.
With whom they don't sleep is often sad information.
Look at your own family: Are parents a unit in a bed-room?

◇◇

One of Katie's secrets, "I've never told anybody," was that last summer at a family reunion, Katie had been molested by an older cousin. "He just touched me is all," she minimized. He had touched her breasts and rubbed her vagina, but she didn't get scared until he tried having intercourse. She cried. He gave up and bargained that if she'd just give him a blow job there'd be no hard feelings. There were no hard feelings.

Katie's Signs

Katie anxiety showed in her *emotional instability*. She'd cry at the drop of a hat, rage at her brothers, talk endlessly on the phone about girlfriend drama, and welcome people in and out of her life with ease. Some moments she was maniacally happy, the family entertainer and everyone's darling. Then without warning, she'd lock herself in her room, sob loudly and long, and write dark, suicidal poetry.

She had an *eating disorder*. She ate in an all or nothing way. For days at a time she wouldn't be hungry and her mom couldn't get her to eat anything, not even her favorites. Then she'd flip and eat everything in sight, whether she liked it or not. Always, she would drink Coke. She loved Coke. Mom also let her have unlimited coffee, which she took black with four sugars.

Sleeping was another anxiety-related problem. (No connection with the caffeine and sugar, I'm sure!) Katie wouldn't go to bed at a reasonable time, always claiming homework. Then she'd stay up too late and be unable to get out of bed in the morning, necessitating mom driving her to school, screeching into the parking lot just as the bell was ringing, whereby Katie would smile beguilingly at the homeroom teacher to escape a tardy slip.

Often at night Katie would have *nightmares*–she'd had them since she was a little girl–and mom would go rushing in and crawl into bed with her. Other nights mom would awaken to find Katie had slipped into bed with her and was sound asleep. Sometimes Katie's brothers would find her on their floor, curled up in a ball with her pillow and blanket. Still other nights Katie slept in her closet behind her clothes. If she did that, she'd close a cat or two in the closet with her. Mysteriously, her closet always smelled like cat pee.

Katie had nightmares, bad dreams, insomnia, horrible day dreams and lots and lots of intrusive thoughts. Someone was chasing her; someone was holding her down; someone was brandishing a knife; someone was cutting her hair. Sometimes she heard a kitten crying, and she was always amazed that no one else could hear it.

Katie's symptoms seemed to congeal and be revealed on her head. When I met her, her hair was purple, but in the course of our therapy it was also orange, blue, pink, green, jet black and platinum blonde. At various times, it was long enough to wear in dreadlocks and short enough to spike.

Her make-up and attire were equally unusual and unpredictable. *She advertised her feelings with her clothes as well as her hair*, seesawing from pink glitter and frilly blouses to long black skirts and long sleeved black shirts, complimented by dark, black eye makeup and black lipstick. It was always an adventure to see if I could recognize her. She never looked the same twice–not even similar. Luckily for the family budget, she and her friends wouldn't have dreamt of shopping anywhere other than Goodwill.

◇◇

Where and how do we each wear our anxiety?
Are you so anxious that you must look perfect?
Are you so anxious that you've given up and look a wreck?
Are you so anxious that you will be criticized that you intentionally give people something to criticize – piercings, tattoos, chains.
Perhaps we can stop judging each other and simply see: anxiety.
We each wear our anxiety.

◇◇

Katie's grades, too, were all over the map, which frustrated the hell out of her educator/father. If she liked the teacher, regardless of the subject, she got an A. Her amount of dislike for a teacher could be accurately predicted by whether she got a C or a D. If she hated the teacher, she got an F, and she earned it.

And, then, of course, there was the symptom that brought Katie into therapy: her *cutting*. The cuts on Katie's arms showed. She wore them like a badge of courage. She made no effort to hide the scars and slashes in various states of redness and healing. The cuts on her tummy and upper legs didn't show.

An issue Katie quickly brought up in therapy was her *sexual orientation*. During the time I knew Katie, she dated straight men, homosexual men, homosexual women and a transgendered person. I just kept reassuring her that her sexual preferences would become clear in time. I suggested she date whomever she wished, gather information about how she felt with each, and make commitments to none.

Also, not obvious to a casual observer or her parents was the knowledge that Katie was a *smoker*. She poached cigarettes from her chain-smoking mama and helped herself to her pot-smoking dad's stash of weed. She was self-soothing and self-medicating, as were both parents. An anxiety-ridden mother who continued to smoke with a breast cancer diagnosis and a posttraumatic stress survivor dad had both role-modeled their coping skills for Katie.

◇◇◇

Parents role-model their coping skills for their children, the good coping skills and the bad coping skills.

◇◇◇

Her Steps

As is very common when a child enters therapy, we had to start with the parents.

Katie had no **boundaries** in her home. No boundaries established when or where she slept, or when and what she ate, or her behavior, which vacillated from intense, emotional dependence to hateful, rebellious independence.

Mom was about to lose her job as full-time mother, a career by which she had identified herself and her raison d'etre. "I don't want to die until my children are raised," she had inappropriately and unfortunately told Katie. The reverse of that statement is, once my children are raised, I'll have nothing for which to live. Also, mom had faced death, was still racing death, and wanted to shower her only daughter with all the love and sympathy she was too angry to give to her husband and too late to give her almost emancipated sons. Mom treated Katie like a baby, and Katie accommodated by acting like a spoiled brat who desperately needed mothering.

Mom showed up alone when I asked the parents to schedule a time. The time mom had selected, early evening, so as not to interfere with dad's teaching schedule, was none-the-less inconvenient for him.

A necessary note on systems theory here. Systems theory–looking at individuals in terms of the system from which they've come, family of origin, and the system in which they currently appear, their present day family–is the theoretical framework of marriage and family therapy. The way that systems theory helps us think about Katie's family is this: It would be easy to conclude that dad is inaccessible and doesn't care about Katie. That would be a lopsided view. It may be true, but it is only one possibility. As I talked to mom, it became clear that she was what used to be called the "telephone operator" in the family. In these days of high tech, I'm not sure that term even makes sense anymore. But, the telephone operator was the one through whom all communication in a family was disseminated. Everyone had to and did communicate with each other through the operator. They could not speak directly. Dad couldn't talk to Katie–he had to talk to mom who talked to Katie and told Katie what dad wanted Katie to know. Or, more accurately, mom told Katie what mom wanted Katie to know of what dad had said. All communication comes through the filter and lens of the operator. In a diagram it would look something like this:

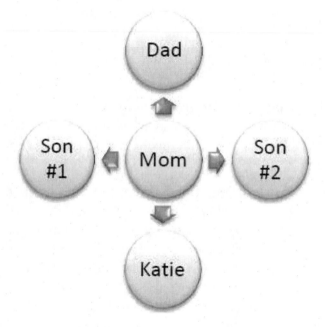

In healthy, functional families, people talk directly to each other.
In unhealthy, dysfunctional families, people talk about each other.

So, mom, for example, might not tell dad when a therapy appointment was scheduled or a tennis meet or a band concert–or might tell him too late. Dad would miss important events, thereby appearing uncaring and selfish. This would allow mom to be the "good" parent and everyone's hero.

Mom was the manager of the money in this family. If she felt an expense was unnecessary, a new tennis racket, for example, word might come back to the son that dad had nixed the expense, even though it was presented to dad, if it was presented at all, as the demand of a spoiled child.

Now, clearly, a therapist doesn't just blurt out, "Oh, my gosh, you're the telephone operator in this family and that is enabling you to be unduly powerful and totally indispensable to everyone else in the family." A great deal more compassion is necessary and deserving for the mom who is fearful of death and dying and also terrified of losing the job she's held for twenty-some years, the job which has defined her. An approach to this would be to help mom carve out a life of her own based on her own deferred dreams. Mom needed reasons to live instead of fears about dying. (See "Story About Life and Death" at the end of Katie's case study.)

Dad clearly needed to be brought into the family system from his present tangential place. He might, for example, be asked to assume responsibility for the tennis schedule or the transportation to Katie's therapy appointments. (This is not likely to be met with joy from mom, since the very act of including dad would be a reduction of power for mom.)

Katie definitely needed boundaries. She needed the type boundaries one might use with a typical three year old: bedtime, lights out, orders to stay in bed, and consequences for bad behavior. The setting of such boundaries required that the parents work together. Katie's obvious first rebellion was going to be the infamous "divide and conquer." We had to head that off at the pass. Only when mom and dad were aligned, on these few things if nothing else, was Katie going to be forced to comply.

Divide and conquer is a child's test to see if he or she can feel secure.
Parents who function as a unit cannot be divided.
Parents who function as a unit cannot be conquered.
Parents who function as a unit act like parents and hold the power.

When children can't divide and conquer, they can relax and be kids.
They can relax because their parents are in charge, so they don't have to be.

◇◇

It wasn't and isn't much of a surprise that **Katie's anxiety was reduced by the addition of some age appropriate limits.** "I guess therapy is working," Katie said, crediting therapy with the relief she got from having parents who started acting like parents. Katie started doing her school work in dad's office, so he could help her if she got stuck. She didn't get stuck. She simply need some structure to force her to sit down, get and stay off the phone, and do the actual work. Since no phone calls were allowed during this time, the diva drama was reduced. Girlfriend drama requires immediate and constant access. Any delay breaks the intensity.

Katie was supervised by dad, who, since he had a job at home in the evenings now, was forced to cut back on his insurance salesman busyness. This freed mom to take a part time job which required evening work. She also joined a book club that met in the evening.

Katie herself filled notebook after notebook with **her writing and her poems**. The writing veered from the darkness of death and dying and self-destruction to brighter more age-appropriate topics. I paid a lot more interest to the brighter poems and gave her a great deal more validation. (If you want a behavior increased, feed it. If you want something to dry up and disappear, starve it.) Katie wrote a long letter to the cousin who had molested her. She didn't know if she wanted to send it to him or not. I suggested she show it to her mom and dad and let them help her decide what action to take. They couldn't protect her, I argued, if they had no idea what was going on.

After I'd seen Katie for about two months, I happened to pass the jewelry counter in a department store and an idea flew into my head. I saw bracelets with four strands of silver intertwined. Four friends. Four strands.

I bought four bracelets and Katie and I concocted a plan. She and the three friends who also cut would have a ceremony and would solemnly swear to tell each other whether they cut and where they cut. If one of them cut herself, the other three would have the option of self-cutting at the same place. They wore the bracelets to remind themselves of their solemn promise to each other that they would do their best to never cut again, since their individual cutting would now impact all four of them. Their fates were intertwined.

Clearly, in retrospect, it's easy to see the number of ways in which this could have backfired. But, it didn't. Their love of drama and the intensity of their feelings stopped the cutting epidemic as quickly as it had started. **They spread "non-cutting" to each other** with as much success as they had spread "cutting."

Katie and I worked on **self-monitoring and accountability**. I suggested a referral to a nutritionist because I saw how easily she could succumb to a full-blown eating disorder. She and I read books, wrote and read poems to each other and became good pals as allowed by the therapist/client relationship. She teetered back into the range of normalcy and went away to college.

My Story

The last I heard Katie is pursuing a PhD in psychology. I hope she works with adolescents. She herself had such a wild ride as a teen that little would shock her and she could relate to almost anything an adolescent brought her.

The tennis player is a bachelor high school teacher and tennis coach. The musician brother is a recovering alcoholic who married an older woman who had a number of children and they run a campground in a distant, warmer, state.

Mom and dad have divorced. Mom is still in remission, devoting herself to her part time job and her volunteering at the synagogue. Dad has gotten active in the veterans' recovery program and volunteers full time at a local veterans' hospital.

Katie taught me a great deal. She taught me not to show my shock. Colored hair, strange hair styles, tattoos, piercings all roll past me now as mere disguises. She also taught me to use what clients bring. It was in the third session that Katie explained that "everybody" was cutting. "Everybody" turned out to be she and her three best friends.

That chance comment turned out to be a vitally helpful piece of information.

Katie was also my finest teacher when it came to learning about cutting. She was so articulate about "letting the pain out." She wrote and talked about the way her anxiety (she used other words, but I got the drift) built and built until she hurt herself. She was instrumental in helping me understand and create some ways to work with this strange and off-putting phenomenon of self-mutilation. Self injurious behaviors, seen as a symptom of anxiety, are much more accessible to treatment and understanding than when seen through other frameworks.

Katie will never be a traditional woman no matter how well educated. She thinks outside the box and she feels outside the box. I hope her therapy and extensive education in psychology help her value herself as the unique and trendsetting person she will always be.

P.S. Katie also taught me a valuable lesson about anti-depressants. Katie took Paxil for two or three years. Paxil is a very good anti-depressant with a viable anti-anxiety component. When she felt stable enough to go off it, her primary care physician told her to just stop taking it. She did, and cried non-stop for two weeks until we put together the medication piece. **Do not stop medication cold turkey**. Wean off it. Slowly. Titrate off. Find a doctor or an experienced professional to guide you. NEVER stop taking medication without telling someone what you're doing. Katie had just stopped, as her family doctor had said, and thinking nothing of it, said nothing to her family or friends. You need an objective observer to keep an eye on you when you start medication and when you stop medication. Treat all psychological medications with great respect.

ALSO, if you live in a four season climate, the only time to go off an antidepressant is in the spring, when the days are getting longer and we have more sunshine. That way nature is on your side. The statistic with which I'm familiar is that 85% of all those who start an antidepressant go off it too soon. Once you start these meds, you need to give your brain chemistry time to adapt to and accept the new normal of actually having and keeping some serotonin in your brain. Again, the statistic with which I'm familiar is that typically one should take an antidepressant for two to five years before trying to stop it. After about 10 years most people develop a tolerance to specific medications and might need to switch from one to another. And, of course, whenever using medication, consult with a physician who is very familiar with that medication. An ounce of consultation might prevent a pound of unnecessary suffering.

Story about Life and Death

In the 1980s I was fortunate enough to attend a week-long workshop on death and dying. The featured speaker was Elisabeth Kubler Ross. Her research on the subject is so extensive and well-respected that she has come to be known as "The Death and Dying Lady." About half the participants at the workshop were doctors, nurses, hospice specialists and therapists who worked with people dealing with end of life issues. The other half of the attendees were people who were terminally ill.

That first night at supper I sat beside a tall, extremely thin and very ill-looking young man. He told me he had AIDS and was trying to decide whether to stay in the east with his mom and die in her home, or go back to the west coast where he had a partner who loved him and wished to care for him as he died. At the beginning of the workshop this young man walked haltingly, bent over his crutches, and stated clearly that he was attending to get advice and guidance on where to die.

At the end of the week-long training this same young man was standing up straight, walking with just a cane, and smiling when he announced that he had decided to return to California to be with his partner for the rest of his life. Clearly, he was still terminally ill. But he had made a perceptual change and was now focused on where to live instead of where to die. Or, as some people say, he had chosen to "live until he died."

PAULA

Her Story

When she entered therapy, she had 13 cats and an invalid mother living in her home. She had two minimum wage, part-time jobs, neither of which used her Bachelor's degree in fine arts. Her van was paid off, but had 180,000 miles on it and was frequently on the fritz, often leaving her stranded and without transportation. She suffered from migraines, serious intestinal problems and panic attacks. At almost 50, she had never married. She had recently met someone who seemed normal enough that she thought perhaps she should get herself into therapy and attend to her anxiety.

"When do you first remember feeling anxious?" I asked. "When I was nine," she replied immediately. "My father left. My sister was three and my mother was inconsolable and all of a sudden, I was in charge."

"What's your mother like?" I encouraged. She started by assuring me that her mother was a good person. (This is always a bad sign. When a new client is immediately defensive of what a good person his or her mother is . . . there is soon going to be reason for an objective listener, me, for example, to start raising her eyebrows at the lack of appropriate mothering said client was given.) Paula's mother was a "good person" who, from the moment Paula's father left, switched her complete and absolute dependency from a grown man to a nine year old little girl–think third grader.

Paula's mother had never worked, so Paula, her mom, and her little sister subsisted on child support. Paula wrote the checks for the household–at nine!–and walked to the grocery store, carrying home whatever was needed that could be afforded. There was, of course, no car and no money for bus fare. Paula took care of her little sister whenever she was home. Paula did the laundry and whatever cleaning got done. She woke herself up for school and walked there each day whatever the weather. When she came home from school, her baby sister, who had been parked in front of the television all day, ran to meet her and demanded to play. Her mother, as if finally off the clock, rose from the living room sofa and took to her bed, from which she shouted orders and dispensed disapproval.

(So far I see no reason for any anxiety, do you?)

Paula got herself through high school and four years of a local college on grants, loans and part-time jobs. Through it all, she cared for her dependent, helpless, insatiable mother and her dependent younger sister. Then she high-tailed it out of town and moved as far away as she could get in the contiguous United States.

She stayed away, happily, working a job she loved, living near her father and stepmother. Until her mother had a stroke. Then Mom called Paula and, using guilt, talked Paula into coming home to resume taking care of her.

Paula cashed out her meager retirement and returned to town. She put a down-payment on a modest older home where her mother could live downstairs, and she could live upstairs. Mom recommenced her invalid, agoraphobic life style, and Paula recommenced her childhood caretaking, complete with its attendant anxiety.

Mom had never allowed pets, so Paula never turned one away. Slowly they came, until at the highest number there were 15 cats and a dog. In addition to these 16 helpless ones, who depended on Paula to clean up after them, Paula's mom's helplessness now extended to lack of bladder and bowel control. Mom spent her days sitting in adult diapers, not bothering to put on any pants; it was too much trouble, as were bras, as was showering or teeth-brushing or face-washing or any other basic hygiene which might encourage social interaction.

So Paula learned to balance her jobs with doctors' appointments for mom. Paula spent hours every week in efforts to make sense of the social security system and the elderly programs for which her mom might qualify.

Paula had no life of her own. Her mother *needed* to know where she was all the time. Her mom's insecurity created a vulnerability which fed her mom's insecurity which created more vulnerability. The vulnerability created fear which led to more vulnerability which led to more fear. Two part-time jobs, 16 pets and a helpless, invalid mother imprisoned Paula in the same negative feedback loop in which her mother was stuck: insecurity, vulnerability, fear, insecurity, vulnerability, fear – anxiety. Debilitating anxiety.

Insecurity creates vulnerability.
Vulnerability feeds insecurity.
More insecurity creates more vulnerability.
Increased vulnerability increases fear.
Increased fear increases vulnerability.
Insecurity, vulnerability, fear – ANXIETY.

And then Paula met Harry at church. They started dating and fell in love. Much to Paula's astonishment, her anxiety now developed into full-blown panic attacks, and she sank into depression. What even moderately healthy man would put up with her life style and her ridiculous responsibilities? She wanted a life of her own and some love. She had all these obligations. She saw no place in her life for her own agenda or her own pleasures. She had nothing extra, no energy, no joy, no time, nothing, to give Harry. She couldn't have a life of her own. She was not entitled.

Her Signs

Paula was *distracted and unfocused.* When talking to her, she moved from topic to topic with *little perceived organization.* Her speech pattern was indicative of her mental functioning. She was *scattered, easily pulled off track, and difficult to follow.* If she were a sentence, you couldn't diagram her.

Paula was *underemployed.* This was a direct result of her anxiety, which made working up to capacity extremely rare, since so much of life's energy was spent "*scanning.*" We talked about this in The Many Faces of PTSD. Those with anxiety can never relax to the task at hand. They are pre-occupied with replaying what they encountered yesterday and fast-forwarding to what might be barely visible on the horizon for tomorrow. They spend a massive percentage of energy constantly on guard, hyper-vigilant, scanning the environment for danger. Their radar is never turned off.

◇◇◇

A major, disruptive sign of anxiety is "scanning."
Anxious people are constantly checking the environment
for danger.
They are like air tower controllers or radiologists.
They are constantly on the lookout for something, any-
thing, that doesn't belong.
Their goal in life is to be able to see things coming from a
long way off.
To accomplish this, they are constantly "scanning."

◇◇◇

Paula was also underemployed as a result of *adverse childhood experiences*, which is what psychologists previously called "abuse and neglect." We also talked about this in The Many Faces of PTSD. Paula has a great deal of resistance to seeing herself as a posttraumatic stress survivor, but she is one, of course. Adverse childhood experiences include all forms of abuse and neglect, including the types Paula endured, which were age-inappropriate responsibilities and neglectful and non-protective parenting. In the early years, when dad was still in the picture, he stayed away from home as much as possible because a crazy lady lived there–the woman he had promised to love and protect and grow old with. Not only did he fail to make good on that contract legally, he failed to uphold that contract morally, and in the process he did not protect his own children from the crazy lady. He fled. He saved himself. In the process, he sacrificed his children.

Without the protection of her father, Paula was left vulnerable to the machinations and malevolence of her mother. (Her mother's story would be a separate issue. Her mother was not born to be a helpless, vulnerable, malevolent, manipulative woman. She, too, had her horrors and her abuses and neglects, whatever they were. She, too, suffers from PTSD. The difference is that Paula's mother became a *victim* of PTSD and never transitioned from victim to *survivor*. When and if, as an adult, one chooses to stay a victim and not work to become a survivor, that is a choice each of us has the right to make. BUT, not if we're parents. If, as parents, we choose to stay stuck in our victim roles, then we keep the dysfunction going through another generation, and that is unconscionable. None of us will ever be perfect parents. My kids will need to seek out therapy as surely as will yours. But since I'm *writing* this book and you're *reading* this book, it won't be because *we didn't try* to be as healthy as possible or because *we chose* to stay stuck.)

A parent has the obligation and responsibility to become
as healthy and functional as possible.
To remain a victim or a dependent adult is to pass on
to the next generation our own boatload of unresolved
issues.
We had no control over what happened to us, but we do
have control over what we choose to do about it.

In my experience, Paula, and people who had similar growing up experiences to Paula's, will all minimize the negativity of those experiences: "Oh, it wasn't so bad. Lots of people had it worse. I didn't get beaten or sexually abused." As Elisabeth Kubler Ross stated, "It doesn't matter if the elephant is standing on your toe or your whole foot." Trauma is an elephant. Trauma is trauma. DO NOT compare your trauma to the trauma of anyone else.

"It doesn't matter if the elephant is standing
on your toe
or your whole foot."
-Elisabeth Kubler Ross

If Paula's abuse had been more obvious, someone, most likely an alert teacher, would have intervened. But an anxious child often presents like a shy child. Why don't we ever stop to think what makes a child *shy* in the first place? Fear, I would say. And where does fear come from? Throw a child up in the air or swing them around and what do they do? They shriek with joy and demand more. "Mo," I have heard my grandchildren beg their daddies. They're fearless. Children who are raised by normal mommies and daddies are without fear and are typically not overly shy. That's because they are protected, treasured, nurtured, read to, played with, sung to, hugged, taught to look both ways before crossing a street and reminded to hold a hand in a parking lot. They are treated like children. They have boundaries to curb their boundless energy and enforced hours of napping and sleeping for rest and restoration.

Normal children are not expected to write the checks for the rent and the utilities. Paula remembers at age nine becoming aware of when bills were due and how long grace periods lasted. She shopped store brands and Goodwill. She learned the bus schedule.

Go check out any other third grader and imagine him or her bearing this level of responsibility and pressure. Anxiety? I should say so. In every fiber and every neuron.

◇◇◇

Children asked to assume age-inappropriate levels of responsibility and pressure are children who will become anxious.

◇◇◇

Now let's add to that a mother who chooses to take to her bed and demand nursing, housekeeping, and health-aide services around the clock, seven days a week, 52 weeks a year. And then factor in a three-year old for whom to care, 24 hours a day, 365 days a year.

Paula learned in third grade that *she was different* from other third graders. She wasn't carefree; she was careful. She didn't ask for lunch money; she knew there was none. (To this day Paula doesn't eat lunch.) She didn't have the latest of everything; she was simply late for everything.

Forty years later, Paula is *overly responsible, easily made to feel guilty, unmindful of her own needs, shy, fearful, easily distracted, underemployed, underpaid, underfed, under focused and underappreciated.*

When you look at Paula, you are reminded of a young girl. She is slight, petite and wears her hair in a ponytail. She works in a service industry and usually works more than 40 hours a week, for no extra pay, never takes a lunch, and until she met Harry, she hadn't had a vacation since she had returned home to care for her mom, 10 years ago.

Paula still *bails her younger sister out of every mess she gets herself into*, which is many messes, *spends money she doesn't have* on her two nephews, *pays her sister's cell phone and cable bills and supplies many of the groceries for her sister's family.* She chauffeurs her nephews back and forth to school and does such jobs as cleaning out the refrigerator or scrubbing the bathroom for her unemployed sister. (Her sister is diabetic, after all, and has high blood pressure.)

When Paula is home, her mother is constantly calling her to "step and fetch." It is Paula who makes the meals, cleans, buys the Depends, and even, on occasion, comes down from her upstairs apartment to change the channel on her mother's television.

The only person Paula *doesn't take care of* is *herself*. Oh, she always looks lovely, stylish, still on Goodwill purchases, clean and organized. But inside, Paula is a nervous wreck.

Her Steps

Paula's new significant other, Harry, brought her to **therapy** with me. He picks up the tab. He is smitten, and it was his idea that they come for counseling early in their relationship. There were a number of pretty obvious potential problems: their 20 year age difference, his children, and her mother, to name the big three.

I knew Harry previously. He and his first wife, Anne, were in marital therapy when she died suddenly, unexpectedly and tragically early, from a massive coronary. In addition to grief over the loss of their mom, Harry and Anne's three daughters, all in their twenties, were traumatized by the sudden death. They were not ready for dad to do anything other than grieve over and revere their dear mother. They had no idea that the relationship was fraught with issues and that things between their parents were not what they had seemed. Harry and Anne had parented well together. They just didn't like each other very much.

Then Harry wants to date a woman 20 years younger than he. What was the old fool thinking? Now, mind you, these girls wouldn't have accepted anyone, let alone someone who looked so non-matronly and was poor. Obviously she was after his money.

So, they hated her, the idea of her, and the reality of her.

Paula's mom, on the other hand, hated Harry. He was positioning himself to require time and attention from her full-time slave. Harry was controlling, blunt and focused. Paula was compliant, soft and slow to accept change. He got things done. She pondered where to start. Her pace frustrated him. His pace scared her. His pace scared her mom, too. Here was a man who was going to change a perfectly good system.

Where in the world does one begin with this?

We started with **the Myers/Briggs Personality Inventory**. (I talked about this in The Many Faces of PTSD, but for those of you who haven't read that book, or for those of you who need a refresher, as well as for those of you for whom this information is falling on virgin ears, here we go.)

The easiest way to understand the Myers/Briggs is to take it yourself. Simply type [Myers/Briggs] in the search box and a few options down is a test sponsored by Humanetrics. It's free. Seventy-two questions. It gives a printout which contains four letters with a number referencing each letter.

◇◇◇

Go online and type [Myers/Briggs] in the search box.
The test provided by Humanetrics is free and reliable.
You'll be given a one-page printout with your personality
type.

◇◇◇

What this test does is divide people into 16 different personality types. These are incredibly helpful for individual therapy and invaluable for marital therapy. The letters and numbers, which correspond to the strength of each variable, tell us what type personality we have arrived in the world wearing.

All of us come wired. We are what we are, and it's all good. No personality type is either bad or unnecessary in the world. And the four temperament divisions into which the personality types are shaped are vital for self-awareness.

The Myers/Briggs is the most used and best researched test in psychology. An estimated two million people take the Myers/Briggs each year. If you look for books about the Myers/Briggs, you'll find at least 1,850,000 options. The book from which I have learned what little I know about this mammoth topic is David Keirsey's Please Understand Me. What I go on to explain about each personality and temperament type is informal information I've gathered over 20 plus years as a therapist.

After you take the test, you'll find yourself with four letters. If your second letter is an "S," you will find either a "J" or a "P" for your fourth letter. This means that your temperament is that of either an SJ or an SP. If your second letter is an "N," you will find either a "T" or an "F" for your third letter. This means your temperament is that of either an NF or an NT. These then are the four temperaments: SJ, SP, NF, NT. It is these temperaments we're going to talk about because they open for us the doors of self- and other-knowledge.

◇◇◇

SJs are the responsible worker bees of the world.
They keep the societal train well-greased and on the track.

◇◇◇

SJs make the world go round. They keep it spinning. They are the rule-followers who do what they should, and they understand the world through their senses. If they can't see it, hear it, taste it, touch it, smell it and feel it (feel in a kinesthetic sense, not an emotional sense), then it doesn't exist to them. That's the "S" influence. The "J" influence is that these people are planners, organizers, and they like to accomplish things in a coherent, consistent, sequential way. (My SJ teacher friend always carries her lunch and always has three things in her lunch: an apple, carrot sticks and a yogurt. She admits that sometimes she takes grapes instead of an apple.)

George Washington and Dwight Eisenhower are two notable SJs. The squirrel, who plans for winter by storing away nuts, and the beaver, who perseveres as he gnaws his way through logs and branches to build his dam home, are animals which represent the SJ. Thirty-eight percent of the population are these traditional, loyal SJs.

Sensing and judging individuals, SJs, are caring but not usually affectionate. They are sensitive, but not usually empathic. Their great strengths are responsibility, honesty and trustworthiness. Their typical weakness is judging and resenting those who are not as predictable, devoted and accountable.

◇◇◇

SPs are the life and energy of the world. They were born to play!
They get off the train for adventures and they love the detours.

◇◇◇

SPs are the polar opposites of SJs. If they can get someone else to handle the drudgery of daily life, they're all for it. The "S" influence is sensing, like the "S" in the SJ. So SPs perceive the world through their senses, too. Like the SJ, the SP is also a realist, but typically SPs define reality differently. SPs usually decide, *really,* what does it matter if we make the beds and do the dishes? They'll just need to be re-done tomorrow, so why stress out about it? Let's eat, drink and be merry.

The "P" of the SP is perceiving. The perceiver, when paired with the sensor, is impetuous, spontaneous and primed for adventure. There is no forethought here. Lights. Camera. Action. John F. Kennedy and Ernest Hemmingway were two well-known and representative SPs. Where SJs are the rule-followers, SPs are the rule-breakers, or at least the rule-benders. Well, actually, it's just that the rules don't apply to *them*! If you're not an SP, get out of the fast lane. The fox is the animal used to portray the SP. Wily, creative, conniving, artistic, often musical and invariably great with their hands, the SP is the name on the wall: for a good time, call. Obviously, a slight down-side to this temperament might be a lack of accountability. Pay the bills? Go to work? Responsibility? Oh, don't be such a stick in the mud. (Does this remind you of Miks's wife Ann in Mike's case study? Ann said, when caught having a sexual relationship with a man other than her husband, "Oh, don't get hung up in the details. Just get over it!")

Seventy-five percent of the world is sensing. The SP, then, also accounts for 38 percent of us. These folks see the world and everything in it as black and white, right or wrong, good or bad. There is no slack to be had from an SJ or an SP. There are no multiple realities or alternative explanations. It is what it is, they will tell us.

The "Ns" of the world, on the other hand, are only 25 percent of the population. "Ns" live in a gray world of abstraction. The "N" temperament is not black and white. Those who are intuitive are subjective thinkers. On tests, for example, they prefer essay questions with unlimited correct answers and lots of room for philosophizing. Sensing, objective thinkers prefer multiple choice and true/false questions. That way it's either right or wrong. No ambiguity. "Ns" are quite comfortable with ambiguity.

◇◇

NTs are the "head" of the world, the architects of ideas.
NTs think outside the box and move society forward.
They design new trains that don't require tracks.

◇◇

NTs are thinkers and analyzers. When intuition is paired with thinking, we get the 12 percent of the population who think outside the box. These folks can visualize the way things have always been done and see new ways to do them. They conceptualize things which have never existed and create the new and different. They are known as "the architects of ideas." The owl is the animal which epitomizes the NT, with its ability to see so much more than the rest of us.

NTs are typically emotionally cool and aloof. They are often arrogant, or at least seen as arrogant, because the niceties of social interaction are meaningless to them. Notable NTs are Einstein and Descartes. Society would sit still and vegetate were it not for these imaginative, intuitive engineers and computer geeks who are responsible for most of the progress of the human race. (Just ask them. They'll tell you!)

◇◇◇

NFs are the "heart" of the world.
It would be a cold, cruel world, indeed, were it not for
their empathy and warmth.
They bring faith, hope and charity along on the train.

◇◇◇

And now we come to the last 12 percent of the population, the NFs. (If you've just added up the percentages to make sure they equal 100, you're either an SJ who is also a "T," or an NT, who is also a "J." If it never occurred to you to add up the numbers, you either don't care–SPs of the world–or wouldn't want to hurt my feelings by adding them up, in case I'm wrong – NFs.)

NFs are the 12 percent of the world who *feel* outside the box, in contrast to the NTs who *think* outside the box. Mahatma Gandhi and Eleanor Roosevelt are well-known NFs, and if any president in recent history was an NF, it would be Jimmy Carter, creator of Habitat for Humanity and Winner of the Nobel Peace Prize. (NFs are very big on peace.) History buffs would tell us that Carter wasn't a very effective president. He wouldn't be. NFs tend to be empathic idealists. They see the potential in people, not people as they actually are. NFs are dreamers, not realists. A job like president of the United States demands realism, savvy, and the ability to make snap, hard, life and death decisions. Don't send an NF.

NFs are the sensitive children. They're the kids who stay in from recess to play with the kid in the cast. They worry themselves sick when the teacher doesn't come to school. They want the admiration and affection of all and give it back twelve-fold.

The dolphin is the animal who represents these soft, make-no-waves dreamers. Faith, hope and charity are what they preach and counsel. Everyone is worthwhile. Criminals had bad childhoods. Let's be green and save the planet for our children. NFs are the hippies who want to make love, not war, and if you have an NF for a friend, you always have someone on your side. NFs will drop what they're doing and rush to your aid, not out of responsibility, like an SJ, but out of love. To the cynic and the realist, NFs are the patsies, the pansies, the naive bleeding hearts.

NF children are described as "too sensitive, too emotional." If these children are protected and sheltered from the harsh and the heartless at a young age, they grow up to be like orchids: indomitable bloomers. But more than any other temperament, NF children need to be coddled and protected in order to grow up to be strong and resilient. If NFs are sheltered early, they grow up to be passionate fighters and tireless crusaders for the sake of humanity, but never for money–NFs are not motivated by money. They're the ones who run the non-profits. But if NF children are not allowed to grow up safe, often their spirits are broken, and they can be traumatized by experiences which other less feeling folks shrug off or gloss over.

SJs need to be taught how to play and be carefree. SPs need to be taught how to be responsible and accountable. NTs typically need some lessons in compassion and social intercourse. If SJs and NTs don't learn their lessons early, they seem to self-correct when their hormones scream out the desire for connection. SPs learn their lessons from a society that demands work if you want a paycheck and bills paid if you want a home or a car. NFs, those highly sensitive people who absorb all life's blows straight to their hearts, need to learn boundaries and reciprocity. They need to grow a shell, or at least a thicker skin.

OKAY . . . back to Paula and her steps.

Paula, it turns out, is an INFP. (This is my profile also, so she and I were able to bond over our shared perceptions of the world.) Harry is an ESTJ, the exact opposite of Paula. He is as concrete as she is abstract. He thrives on people; they wear her out. She makes decisions in her heart, based on relational issues, and he makes decisions in his head, based on logic and irrefutable evidence. He is organized to a fault, and she has learned to go with the flow. He puts self-care first, and she never seems to get to self-care. He's always trying to make plans a couple of months in advance, buy airline tickets, for example, since they're cheaper in advance. She's reluctant to commit to a plan for tomorrow, much less to say she'll do something next March. Clearly, no one is wrong and no one is right in these Russian standoffs. Paula and Harry simply perceive the world differently.

So . . . we started with the logical conclusion that **they were different** and looked at **the ways in which they were different**. Remember, my mentor Phil always said, "If you can name it, you can tame it."

◇◇◇

"If you can name it,
you can tame it."
–Phil Hochwalt

◇◇◇

I didn't have to sell Paula and Harry on **the idea that "opposites attract."** That simply made them smile smugly. As I frequently say to couples, the one thing therapy can't help with is the magic and mystery of chemistry. Chemistry they had. So we worked on **understanding, aware-ness, tolerance and acceptance**. And we started with a **shared vocabu-lary** which allowed us to "name" the differences in a non-judgmental way. From a pacing standpoint, we needed to **slow Harry down and speed Paula up**. It became a strange dance, his four steps to her one and his straight path to her circuitous one. But dance they have for the last four years. They agree on where they're headed, to marriage and full-time cohabitation. How to get there is a constantly evolving process.

Harry's daughters have not given an inch. So, Harry has a separate relationship with them, with separate visits and separate communication. Paula would like to be included, but isn't so far. Two of the girls are polite at family functions; one of them refuses to speak. I would guess it might be a tragedy of some sort that brings Paula in, since her great strength is her incomparable empathy and compassion.

Paula's mom has had an actual health crisis, the result of which was placement in a nursing home. Paula could never have *made* it happen, but when it happened on its own, she was ready. **Paula moved her mom from the hospital to a nursing home** and she remains adamant. "You can't come home, mom. I can no longer care for you." Mom insists that all of this hard-heartedness on Paula's part is Harry's influence. All that accusation does is incense Paula and make her hold the line.

Harry and Paula have **started travelling** and, surprise of all surpris-es, when they are away, alone together, they have a fabulous time. When Paula is in a respectful and protected relationship, her anxiety calms down. When Harry is free of the outside forces with which to fight, he has no need to be controlling.

Paula and I have done a lot of work on **understanding her anxiety**, what it is, how it started, how it gets triggered, and how she might reduce it and how to begin to control it. She has tried **breathing exercises, yoga, meditation, walking, journaling and more breathing**. Interestingly, the more she establishes boundaries with her mother and her sister, the greater reduction in anxiety she experiences.

I have also worked extensively with Harry on his anxiety – which is that Paula will never break free of these maternal and sisterly restraints, and he will never be able to have a full-time wife and companion. The more he can manage his own anxiety, the less he feels he has to control Paula and her decisions, which are always slower than his. He sees it, he does it. She sees it, she thinks about it, mulls it over, and looks at it from every which way.

Harry's anxiety also rises when he concentrates on how old he is and how slowly Paula tends to move. His anxiety reduces when he concentrates on how far they've come and how deeply they share their common goal. **Paula is teaching Harry patience. Harry is teaching Paula hope. They are teaching each other to believe in love.**

My Story

Paula's anxiety has been difficult to treat. She has no memory of living without anxiety. I've had a hard time convincing her that she and her anxiety are actually separate. The travelling she has done with Harry has been the most telling example to her that she no longer needs to be on high alert all the time. She can function and focus on the future as well as live fully in the enjoyment of the present.

Harry's anxiety, which is so heightened when Paula dithers and dallies and rescues her mom and her sister, also reduces dramatically when he and Paula are away together. He tells me she is a different person, kind of wild and free and impetuous but also level-headed and imperturbable when they encounter travel snafus. A decrease in her anxiety immediately decreases his.

I remind them all the time that their most anxious moments are triggered by others. Paula's work, where everyone wants a piece of her, and interactions with her family, who each want a slice of her, keep her from moving forward more quickly. She sets aside a day to clean out the attic or the basement. (I think I forgot to mention that Paula is a packrat – or even perhaps a hoarder.) But seemingly anytime Paula sets aside time for herself either her mother or her sister has an emergency. Her mom needs a sympathy card, which Paula must go out and purchase at this very moment (or perhaps someone will die – lol) and her sister has the flu and must have immediate help with the children.

Paula's anxiety makes her unavailable to Harry. Her unavailability triggers his anxiety. Interestingly enough, Harry's first wife was emotionally cold and unavailable. (I suspect his mother was also.)

I also remind Paula and Harry, who met in church, that their souls have chosen each other, so they can each learn the soul lessons they need to learn here on earth.

(Or, as Tari, my friend and fellow-therapist says, "We have much to learn here in earth school.")

The Harville Hendrix book, <u>Getting the Love You Want</u>, explains how we are attracted (wildly, sometimes) to a person who embodies the negative characteristics of our parents. Our unconscious minds (or as some of us think of it, our souls) know that we will be free to progress to new soul heights if we can work through these old lessons from the past in our present relationships – control, anger, abandonment, betrayal, abuse, suffocating "love", jealousy, etc., etc.

Paula and Harry are progressing as I write this. We count the markers of movement, and I caution them both to stay out of anxiety and to stay focused on the amazing gift of their love for each other.

The pets are down to four, two of which now live at Harry's house. Paula and Harry spend five or six night a week at his house. They throw parties there, and he cooks, and she decorates. One of his daughters has come around, one is ambivalent and one is still openly hostile.

Progress. Movement. Life is a process.

◇◇

LIFE IS A PROCESS. A PROCESS.
LIFE . . . . . is a PROCESS.

◇◇

And, when all else fails, I remind them of Paul's advice in Galatians:

"Be anxious for nothing."

Be anxious for nothing.

No anxiousness.

For nothing.

HERB

His Story

Herb came into therapy for anxiety, referred by a respected psychiatrist who had started him on medication and then sent him for counseling. Herb sought out the psychiatrist because his boss at work gave him an ultimatum: Get help or get out.

Herb was a man in his 50s who had been married once, briefly, and had no children. He was tall, slender, good-looking and liked women.

Herb was a computer geek. He was incredibly smart, and he knew it. He owned and lived in an investment property which he was trying to restore so he could rent out the other three units. He earned over $100,000 a year at work and was employed by a stable and prospering company.

But Herb's temper kept getting him in trouble. He explained to me that anyone would be frustrated with his work situation. The bosses didn't know what they were doing. (Boy, if I had a dollar for every time I've heard that!) His bosses were administrators, not tech savvy, only worried about the bottom line (money, of course), gave out orders that didn't make sense and axed suggestions that Herb made which would have kept things running more smoothly. They would put him in charge of a project and then tie his hands behind his back and insist that he do the project the way they wanted it done.

The company was just toxic, he concluded. He had a boss with whom he'd gotten along great, but that boss had left to go to another company. That's probably what he should do too, Herb said.

But (the always present BUT), his ex-wife still owned half of the investment property, and he wasn't in a financial position to buy her out. He'd only been at his present job nine months. Before that he'd been out of work for about a year. It was hard at his level of expertise, he informed me, to find appropriate employment opportunities.

Barely into the first session he was already "losing me in logic and baffling me with bull shit."

I tried a different tactic. "Tell me about your family and about growing up."

"The old man," he started . . . . That's always a bad sign. Two reasons alert me why it's a bad sign. Number one, almost universally people start with their mother when asked about their growing up. Secondly, in the first session of therapy, most people don't start bashing a parent with demeaning descriptions. Herb was not a usual client.

Herb's father was an alcoholic. Herb remembered being sent to bars by mom to drag his father home. He remembered beatings. Lots of them. The beatings were administered for all kinds of imagined infractions, like not doing things he hadn't been asked to do and not being able to produce things–a bottle of whiskey, let's say–that they didn't have at their house. And Herb remembered nothing but poverty.

At school his teachers liked him, but the kids didn't. He was from the wrong side of the tracks, and he didn't have the right clothes. While other kids were in Boy Scouts and sports, he was home with his mom, helping her and hurting with her.

Herb had an older brother with whom he had lost contact and an older sister, whom, he said, "adored him." He talked to his sister every couple months. He "adored" his niece and nephew, although he couldn't remember how old they were or what they were presently doing. He hated the controlling bastard his sister had married.

He didn't know if his dad was dead or alive. He didn't care if hisdad was dead or alive. No one had heard from dad since that time, about 35 years ago, when dad had gotten mad at mom and beaten her, leaving her for dead. Dad wisely disappeared that day and never had resurfaced.

Herb found his practically unresponsive mother and ran next door to use a telephone and call the paramedics. They hurried her off to the hospital. No one considered that this tall, lanky teen had no way to get to the hospital himself. He remembers running the three miles to the hospital so he could fill out her admission papers.

When she was released a week and a half later, Herb remembers their slow walk home, his half-carrying her. Once he got her home, he went out and got a job.

So, Herb, that lonely, shunned, abused child, grew up to be a lonely, bitter man with a very heavy chip on his shoulder. Here was a mind that should have been nurtured and encouraged, a tender heart that might have learned to be loving and compassionate. But this was not what life had in store for Herb, and given the vagaries of genetics and environment, this was not what Herb was able to choose for himself, either. Herb had no resiliency.

And the more I learned, the sadder the story became. Herb continued to lose his temper at work. Finally, he crossed a line and threatened someone's life in one of his rants. He was fired.

It became apparent that Herb's temper and threats were longstanding problems when he told me more about his ex-wife. She was a painter who showed and sold her work at craft fairs. They met and married when they were both in their forties, a first marriage for each. Herb believed in her without reservation and did all the schlepping for her, to and from their apartment, to and from the car, to and from the fairs. He helped her set up her booths, talked up her work, collected the money, and then loaded everything up and took it home again for her.

While Herb was at work, she met another unappreciated and misunderstood artist on E-Harmony. (What was a married woman doing on E-Harmony, we might ask?) One day when Herb came home from work, he discovered that her artist colleague had schlepped Herb's wife and all her art to his studio.

Herb, never one to suffer an injustice in silence, harassed the artist couple so much that they filed a restraining order. Herb bought himself a gun at that point, believing as he did and still does, that anyone capable of filing a restraining order was capable of hunting down and killing someone.

Then he told me about the strangers loitering around his rental property apartment building. He made frantic calls to the police when people knocked on his door, parked outside his building, shouted at him in the night and even broke his windows.

He was driving one night when a woman rear-ended him. When he got out of the car, he was pistol-whipped, robbed and then tossed back in his car. He told me he never went to the hospital or filed a police report. He was afraid.

This simply didn't add up and his story did not gel for me. I found myself shaking my head, wondering what the missing pieces were. He was so aggressive and so bitter. He had a hair-trigger fuse and a raging temper. People were after him. He was being followed and hounded by strangers. "Everyone" knew where he lived. He wasn't safe. He had no money. He couldn't keep a job or a wife. He was scared out of his wits.

Well, I'm sure you guessed it before I did. He was addicted to drugs and had been on and off for years, working his way from pot to heroin to crack cocaine. It took Herb about eight sessions to finally give me the central piece of the puzzle which brought the picture into focus.

His Signs

Herb had been a geeky, awkward child who had carried the legacy of an *addictive personality and victimhood* into his adulthood.

To say that Herb was high-strung would have been a great understatement. He had a history of shouting matches, fist-fights and restraining orders. He also had an uncanny sense of eleventh hour last chances. But, of course, *uncanny instincts and intuitions* are par for the course for adults who suffered childhood trauma.

Childhood trauma, or adverse childhood experiences, or childhood abuse and/or neglect, whatever terms you want to apply, are the very natural precursors of anxiety.

◇◇

A child is traumatized or abused.
That child wants to avoid future trauma and abuse.
Therefore, that child tries to pay attention to what causes him to be traumatized or abused.
Surely, if the child can pay attention well enough*, he can prevent future trauma or abuse.*
This paying attention well enough *often becomes anxiety.*

◇◇

Herb, for example, realized that he did not get beaten every time his father was drunk. But, he realized that every time he did get beaten, his father was drunk. When Herb's father got drunk, he got loud, belligerent, authoritarian, demeaning, mean, pushy and rude.

Okay. So, Herb needed to be wary of drunk, loud, belligerent, demeaning, mean, pushy, rude people. Herb installed in himself a radar system with which he constantly scans the environment for people with any of these characteristics.

The only time Herb can stop scanning and turn off his radar system is when he is alone. It is impossible to be alone while in a relationship, or at school, or at work, or at the grocery store, the cleaners or the library. So, the tiny Asian man at the dry cleaners who speaks loudly so as to be heard over the noisy equipment appears on Herb's radar as: **Threat.** The boss who shouts, "Staff meeting," appears as: **Threat.** The driver who yells, "Watch where you're going," appears as: **Threat.**

Threats. Danger. More threats. More danger. Where is he safe? Where can he relax? Not even at home, alone. Someone might be parked outside on the street. The phone might ring. The doorbell might chime.

Some rowdy teenager might throw a rock through his window. Even the innocent wind in the trees might sound like a moaning, groaning woman. The wind might even sound like a gasping, unconscious woman who has been beaten by her husband and left for dead.

Herb had no doubt *inherited a predisposition to anxiety*. Surely it is more likely than not that Herb's mom, who married an abusive alcoholic, was an anxious woman. Herb's dad self-medicated with alcohol. What was he self-medicating for? Depression and/or anxiety would be the educated guesses.

Anxiety, remember, is that out-of-whack, things aren't okay, sense of dread and upset which can make us feel certifiably crazy. Crazy enough, in fact, that the few minutes of relief as cocaine takes you outside and beyond your own body and mind might be deeply relaxing. They might be a few stolen moments of not needing to monitor the radar.

But anytime you let up on that radar monitoring, you have to go back at it more seriously than ever. You might have missed something while you were away.

Such is the cycle of anxiety.

Herb had every sign of anxiety I've ever seen, culminating in *paranoia* and a cocaine *addiction*. He was a charming man with a brilliant mind and a handsome shell. None of this could compensate for or stand a chance against his lifelong brain malfunctions caused by a hyper-alert, *overworked nervous system* and a *lonely, terrified heart*.

His Steps

We spun our wheels for the first six or seven sessions. Every time I'd see Herb, it would occur to me to talk to him about transferring to a therapist who could be of more help. Something always held me back. Then that session came where he said, simply, "Okay. I have decided I can **trust** you." The rest of the story came tumbling out and everything started making its own irrational and tragic sense.

Herb admitted he was a drug addict. **Herb knew what he had to do**. It took three tries that I knew of before he was able to go longer than twenty-four hours without "using." We talked about triggers, and his unrelenting trigger when anyone tried to tell him what to do (like his dad) and his unfailing trigger of a helpless victim woman (like his mom) as well as any feelings of vulnerability or incompetence (which his "stupid" bosses seemed to engender).

He actually figured out what to do to give himself a period of time with **lessened triggers.** (We weren't aiming for an absence of triggers. Let's be real.) **Intense physical labor** helped him to quiet the screeching radar. He built a retaining wall at his rental property. It was summertime, it was hot, it was handy, it was heavy, and it engaged his mind and body in something productive.

◇◇

Intense physical movement,
exercise for the sake of exercise,
or exercise for the sake of accomplishing a project,
is the number one most natural and helpful way
any of us can reduce our anxiety.

◇◇

Exercise and hard physical labor can be absolutely meditative. Yoga, tai chi, walking meditation, hiking, jogging, rock climbing all are excellent balm for the anxious spirit.

Herb built a wall and actually, to my amazement, joined a **yoga class** with a female friend. They did yoga and coffee twice a week.

Herb tried his best to **stop using** cocaine. For the most part he used here and there, but he used more sporadically and considerably less, which helped him feel more sane and grounded and in control of his life, as well as giving him money for wall supplies and yoga and coffee.

This lessening of the addiction helped him **calm his raging temper,** and we got to do some **work on perception.** His perceptions were horribly skewed toward paranoia. We talked about **understanding the neutrality of almost all communication.**

The man in the dry cleaning shop who said, "Put dirty laundry here," was speaking loudly because the laundry machines made a racket, not because he was shouting at Herb. And he said, "Put dirty laundry here," because that was where the dirty laundry went, not because he was trying to boss Herb around. I asked Herb to hang around the shop a little bit and see if that wasn't the way the guy behind the counter talked to everyone. Herb was amazed by the results of his data collection.

Then we talked about road rage, and I brought in some of my grandson's Matchbox cars. I asked Herb to drive a car around my coffee table, and as he drove I kept getting in his way. I tried to separate out for him that he wasn't mad at me, Susan, he was mad that someone, anyone, was going to the place in the road where he was intending to go. It wasn't about me. He was focused and knew where he was heading and anyone or anything that got in his way made him angry. It could have been a cow or a dog or a baby carriage. Or a car driven by Lady Gaga or Mother Theresa. **Road rage is about the rager**, he who loses his or her temper, not the ragee, the unwitting victim of our rage who couldn't read our mind and stay out of our way.

◇◇

When we get angry and lose our temper, that anger is about us and our inability to deal with change.
We aren't angry at Billy, our son, who didn't take the trash can to the curb.
We're angry because we wanted the trash can on the curb.
We had it all organized. Now we have been thwarted.
We were in control and someone or something didn't cooperate.
We were pulling out to pass when the car in front also pulled out. Our plan was ruined. We have to adjust and adapt.
We are not omnipotent and omniscient. DAMN!!!!!
How dare the world not do what we want when we want it? Most of us have parents who help us learn to get over ourselves by about the age of three!

◇◇

Herb and I did a lot of **grief work**. His heart was terribly heavy with the unfairness of his mother's unfulfilled life and the injustice of his wife's absconding from their marriage. In neither case had he felt he had any control or any chance to change the outcome. The only two women he had ever trusted in his life had left him. One left through an impossibly early death, and one left through an impossibly hasty change of heart. Both abandonments were beyond his comprehension.

Unfairness is such a hard thing to grasp when you are the one who has suffered the unfair blows. It's as hard as forgiveness when you are the one who needs to be doing the forgiving.

Herb ended up going off the cocaine for about six weeks, or at least that's what he reported to me. In that time period he got a job interview in a neighboring state, sent in all his applications and resumes, bought a new suit, got a real haircut, and flew off to the interview with the company paying for his travel and hotel. He was interviewed that next day, offered the job on the spot, and that very night, before he was to go back in the morning to sign employment agreements and choose insurance plans and so on, he celebrated his good fortune with some cocaine. The next morning he realized he was too strung out to go back to his opportunity.

At that point I believe he gave up on himself. He flew home with his tail between his legs. Herb wrote me a note telling me what happened and cancelling all future appointments.

My Story

I suppose every therapist has to learn from someone the unrelenting power of addiction. If it were easy to break free from an addiction, it probably wouldn't even be called an addiction.

Herb is no doubt still fighting his valiant fight against anxiety, addiction, and his own mind and body. After such prolonged use of cocaine and such harm done to his brain, by not only the drugs, but also by living in a continual state of hyper-alertness, Herb, at almost 60, must look and feel much more like a man in his 80s. I will not be surprised, but I will be saddened, when I read his obituary in the paper. If, indeed, there is anyone in his life who will care enough to put it in the paper.

The life-long pain and poverty that result from early childhood trauma and abuse are immoral and tragic. Herb was a man with a gift of intelligence and reason, a heart of tenderness and compassion, and all of it was wasted. He could never fulfill his destiny, could never become what he might have been because as an innocent child he wasn't protected and nurtured. His mother and father made a tangled mess of their lives, their marriage and their parenting. Some children survive and thrive despite such parents. Herb was not one of the survivors.

Months after I had last heard from Herb, my four-year-old granddaughter, Mikayla, whom we call Mickey, was having a sleepover with me. It was 11:30 p.m. and both she and I were happily in REM dreams when the phone rang. I answered and was told by the therapist who was manning the pager at work that a very desperate-sounding man named Herb had just called on the emergency line and was requesting that I call him back right away.

I looked over at Mickey's sweet head, her hair framed on the pillow, her long brown eye lashes laying gently on her cheeks, her deep, soft breath coming out from between her lips, and I dialed the phone.

Herb answered the phone and he was crying so violently it was difficult to understand what he was trying to tell me. "They" were coming to get him, it was "all over." "They" were going to kill him. He might as well just use his gun and kill himself.

I turned on the bedside light and gently rubbed Mickey's back while Herb poured out his agony. Mickey was sound asleep. She didn't need me to rub her back. I needed to connect with her, to let her safe, happy, protected life ground me.

For an hour and a half Herb raged and cried and begged and promised. I tried to keep him talking, hoping he'd talk himself down from what I could only assume was a very bad trip.

Finally, Herb was more calm and said he didn't hear anyone outside any more. Maybe they had gone. Maybe he could sleep now. Maybe they believed he wasn't there.

He hung up. I turned out the light and snuggled back into bed and put my hand under my pillow. Almost immediately a small, soft four-year-old hand felt for mine and I fell asleep holding hands with Mickey, grateful beyond all gratitude for the gifts of innocence and love on this stormy, dark night.

RETE

Her Story

Her name was Marguerite, but everyone just called her Rete. It was a short, snappy name, and it suited her.

She was the second of three children born to a domineering father who had to be in control of everything and a very unhappy, unhealthy mother who was willing to be submissive in all things.

Dad was career military, which meant that every few years they packed up and set off for a new Marine base. Mom was career servant, which meant that wherever they went, she immediately had the house and the kids unpacked and running like clockwork.

Rete's dad did an inspection every morning before he left for work, another when he returned from work in the late afternoon and then an extensive perimeter check before bed. Nothing and no one was going to invade his home and scare or harm his wife and children. And, except for him, himself, nothing ever did.

Unfortunately, no matter where they lived, the enemy was omnipresent. Dad wasn't sexually abusive, but he was personally invasive. He burst into the bathroom if someone's shower took more than the allotted three minutes. He stormed into their bedrooms if lights weren't out on time. Dimes had better bounce off the freshly made beds or everything, including the mattress, was stripped and flung, as was the offending child, to the corners of the room.

Dad insisted on discipline, silence (speak only when spoken to), and chores. Every Saturday the house or apartment was cleaned thoroughly, toothbrushes used on the bathroom tile, bleach, soap, and more elbow grease than children possessed, used on everything else. "Cleanliness may be next to godliness," as the old saying goes, but this level of obsession was nothing but hell.

◇◇◇

Too much of a good thing,
for example obsessive cleanliness,
is not a good thing.
Overly sanitized surroundings create sterility, not sanity.
For good health, we all need some dirt.
In 25 years as a therapist, no one has ever landed in my
office because their growing-up home was dirty. But I
have witnessed a lot of tears over the fact that "you could
eat off the bathroom floor," but she *never had time for us.*

◇◇◇

Dad ruled by brute force; Mom cried a lot. Mom lived in fear of her husband's temper and criticism. She relentlessly hounded the children in an effort to protect herself by having everything done to his specifications and thus giving him nothing to criticize. Unfortunately, people who are critical don't criticize because something is wrong. They criticize because they are critical people. If nothing is obviously wrong, they'll devise less obvious things. One woman told me her husband used to criticize her for "smiling" too much.

Mom, instead of being comforted by dad's compulsive checking and intense security measures, picked up on the fear which caused the checking and tight security. She was sure danger lurked around every corner, and her view of people was dismal. They were either rotten or lazy, and some were lazy-rotten. Children had to be guarded so as not to be kidnapped. Rape and robbery were epidemic. And the weather? The weather was out to get them, too. Mom and kids spent many a cloudy, rainy afternoon hunkered down in some dark corner **in case** a tornado or thunderstorm might pop up. A knock on the door would have mom shushing the kids and they would all freeze in silence until whoever had knocked gave up and went away. No one was safe anywhere.

The others on the base were going to move on soon, too, so why bother getting to know anyone? The kids weren't allowed to go to other people's homes because they were no doubt dirty, and you could never tell what language those people might use, and they might not pray before dinner, and, of course, there were always worries of rapes and molestations and bad weather. It was safer to just stay home.

School was freedom for Rete. She participated in every extra-curricular activity she could get away with. And she could get away with most things having to do with school, as long as those things didn't cost money. Money, of course, was to be saved, not spent.

Rete's sister was a "kiss up," and Rete's brother was considerably younger than the girls and was his mom's favorite and his dad's second in command. Men had different rights and responsibilities than women. So, little Frankie got to help with the security precautions and the reconnaissance missions while the three females cooked, cleaned and tried to follow procedure.

Rete made friends everywhere she went. She was a natural athlete and when released from lock down, she was a girl looking for a good time. Her spirit was indomitable, her willpower incredible, and she was not about to be beaten by anything outside her own home. She could best anyone's time or batting average or SAT score.

Show her the challenge, and she'd take it and then do anything necessary to conquer it.

But what Rete learned about people was that every few years they left you, and the ones who stayed you pretty much wished had left as well. Rete's parents, Mr. Intimidation and Mrs. Guilt, might have had their temperaments softened by grandparents and aunts and uncles and steady neighbors, but their career military life left in Rete a loud, overwhelming hatred of authority and an intolerance for victimization.

Rete didn't know what she wanted to do for a career when she started college, but she knew she'd have fun getting there. Scholarships got her tuition paid and she landed a job working for the athletic department, so she had extra money to join a sorority and chase some excitement.

She quickly realized that psychology was a breeze for her. She'd been in training all her life and understood the human psyche pretty damn well. Because money meant nothing to her–she was disgusted with the way her parents worshipped it–she started the social work program and realized she was a natural. She could empower people. She had spent her whole childhood empowering herself.

Rete had many friends and boyfriends. Her friends teased her that the boyfriends were "disposable," she threw them away so fast. Until she met Ben in her junior year. Ben was a good old boy from the south, as laid back and fun-loving as was Rete. They also shared that total personality change when competition of any kind was mentioned. Ben was in college on a golf scholarship and Rete, who had never golfed in her life, broke 100 her first time out and fell immediately in love with both Ben and golf. They were married a week after graduation.

Twelve years later Ben was a golf pro and Rete worked part-time as a probation officer. They had three kids and thoroughly enjoyed their home life, both as spouses and parents.

It seemed Rete's childhood of physical abuse and unrelenting criticism was a thing of the past. She was adored by her husband, loved by her kids, respected by her colleagues at work, and feared by her parolees, who knew petite, beautiful Rete was " a force to be reckoned with."

All her life Rete had worn a layer of protection to keep her from buckling under the weight of her mother's emotional berating and beating. Her dad had mellowed over the years, retiring from the Corps and accepting a fairly stress-free job as a private security guard. Her mom had not mellowed, and now that her dad had some health problems and had lost a lot of his bluster, Rete's mom took over the reins. Mom, who was always submissive, became dominant, and dad, who was always dominant, became submissive. Dad had ruled with clean-cut force. Mom ruled with manipulation, subterfuge, guilt and insatiability.

◇◇

Virginia Satir, the mother of marriage and family therapy, said that the model for dysfunctional relationships is that of a dominant partner and a submissive partner.
The model for a healthy relationship consists of two fairly equal partners.
Her classic book People-making *and/or a PBS series entitled*
Communication and Congruence *are excellent resources.*

◇◇

Mom and Dad had settled down "back home" where they had met and where their families still lived. As a child, Rete had never gotten to know either side of her extended family, but as an adult, she became close to and devoted to mom's aging parents. When Rete's grandma was hospitalized with congestive heart failure, Rete put the kids in the car and drove the four hours "home" to surprise her grandparents. She decided to stay in a hotel with the kids since no one knew she was coming and everyone was busy with grandma. She arrived at the hospital, happy to have made it home while grandma was still living and proud of herself for getting her plans worked out so well and so quickly.

Rete's two aunts, her mom's sisters, were in the hospital room when Rete arrived and Rete returned hugs from each aunt as well as hugging her mom and her grandparents. Rete's mom wasn't speaking to either sister, but they were all present and putting on a show for grandma.

Rete visited and then left to return to the hotel to get the kids some supper. She said she'd be back in the morning. Before she even got out of the hospital parking deck her phone rang and her mother, irately screaming, called her everything imaginable. She had talked to her aunts and made her, her mother, look bad by not letting her know she was coming and by staying in a hotel. Rete's mom told her she was "ungrateful, disloyal, a bitch, a trouble-maker," and her mother "wished she'd never been born."

Unfortunately when packing for the trip, Rete had neglected to pack her armor. She hadn't needed it for years. She rarely went anywhere without Ben, and her mother was totally intimidated by Ben. Rete's mom actually believed Ben adored her. In truth, he hated her guts and despised what she'd done to Rete, but with his southern charm and good manners, he always kept that under wraps.

Rete returned to the hotel sobbing and shaking. It was the first time her children had ever seen her cry. When she got back to her own safe home the next afternoon, her first order of business was to find herself a therapist. Apparently her traumatic childhood wasn't as locked up and sealed away as Rete had wanted to believe. There were a few loose ends that Rete needed to tie up.

Her Signs

Rete is a *head-picker*. Rete told me that her beautician told her that an amazing number of people pick their heads. They get any little pimple or blemish, and they start picking, and they won't let the sore heal. The hairdresser knows this from the pain she sees her clients endure when they get chemicals and hair products on their open sores.

Rete only picks her head when she's sitting still. If she's moving in some way, exercising or cleaning or playing sports, she's fine. If she sits down and starts thinking, she starts picking. Rete believes her head-picking to be her #1 indicator of her level of anxiety. She knows she picks her head when she is criticized or attacked in any way. She realizes that when her "inner child" is assaulted, her reaction is to begin picking on herself.

Let's look at a self-mutilating behavior like head-picking. You see, if we can beat others to it, pick on ourselves first, put ourselves down first, hurt ourselves first, we may be able to avoid having to be picked on or put down or hurt by others. And even if they do start assaulting us, we've already begun the assault ourselves and so, at least, we won't have to endure the surprise.

Rete's head-picking may remind you of Dora from her case study and the way Dora cut herself with a knife. Both are self-mutilation. Both are attempts at self-protection. Both are begun, the picking or the cutting (or so many other self-harming activities), in an effort to move us along the cycle of anxiety. Always, we're trying to get the onslaught over, whatever it may be, and it runs the gamut from neglect to abuse of all kinds. Only when we get the onslaught over can we move on to relief.

Rete *exercises excessively*. Ben, a professional athlete, cross-trains and stays in excellent physical condition. It's his job! Rete exercises more frequently, more intensely, and more self-abusively than Ben. It's not unusual for her to be in serious pain the day after a run or a weight lifting session. When she runs on a treadmill, she told me, she frequently sets the elevation at the highest level. For weeks after the last "bombing" by her mother, Rete was running straight uphill and punching into the air in front of her while doing it. While Rete will tell you that her head-picking is her #1 indicator of how high her anxiety is, she'll also tell you that her exercise insanity is her #1 way of trying to reduce her anxiety before it gets a hold of her.

Rete knows her *excessive exercising is another form of self-abuse*. She says she often hears a voice in her head prodding her on when she starts thinking about quitting. The voice invariably says, "You're not hurting yet, so keep going."

◇◇

Exercise has long been touted as the "best natural anti-depressant."
Exercise is also the best natural way to reduce and control anxiety.
Exercise produces endorphins and relieves tension.
Exercise induces self-esteem and a sense of well-being.

◇◇

Rete has *almost no friends*. She has a great many acquaintances, but she is *unable to trust* and *unable to tolerate being vulnerable and intimate*. Ben is her one notable exception and her best friend and confidant. Aside from Ben, Rete is a great buddy, fun to hang with, but she doesn't want and can't relax into any deep friendships. Her experiences with being stabbed in the back are too many. Honestly: if you can't trust your own mother, who can you trust?

Rete *fears nothing*. She knows this is not necessarily a good thing. She will not back down from anything or anyone, and she admits that Ben really worries she'll get herself hurt. She has been known to take on people twice her size if they offend her or are rude and nasty to someone she's with.

For example, a man walked out in front of her car as she was driving down the street, and he banged on her fender because he thought she almost hit him. She slammed on the brakes and got out of the car and started cussing him out. He screamed at her, calling her a crazy bitch and she started moving toward him. He turned and walked away.

She is also fearless about going into hellholes and hovels in pursuit of her parolees. She fearlessly drags them back where they belong. She explains that when you grow up in constant fear inside your own home, the outside world, and physical danger in particular, don't seem very daunting. (I remember a client telling me that when he was 10 he was put on a bus in Ohio and sent to New York City to spend the summer with his 21- year-old uncle. His uncle was a bartender who worked evenings and into the wee hours. My client, a 10-year-old child, would wander the streets of the city while his uncle worked. "I felt safe," he assured me. I always wondered how unsafe things had to have been inside that apartment for that little boy to have felt more safe on the streets of New York.)

To aid in her fearlessness, *Rete is obsessed with looking strong*. She dresses to show off her muscles. She's not trying to look seductive, she's trying to look intimidating. She wants people who see her to know that she is not to be messed with.She wants anyone who encounters her to know she'll "take them down." She admits ruefully that she frequently practices on Ben. She figures that as long as she can take him down, she stands a good chance with anybody. "It's a protective issue," she explains. Rete protects herself by flaunting a body that looks as strong as her mind is.

Rete *wears psychological armor* anytime she's away from her own immediate home and family. She has two primary defense postures: #1, the observer; and #2, the fun girl. Rete, as observer, scopes out a room and tells herself how on guard she must be. Whether at court with her job, at the kids' school functions, or at Ben's golf tournaments, Rete is formal, reserved, listening politely and respectfully and quite approachable. But she gives nothing of herself to anyone. She is behind glass.

The fun girl is the one Ben's friends know, the party hearty, let's-have-a-great- time girl. Everybody loves Rete because she's funny and witty and charming. People can criticize her now for all she cares, because there is nothing personal going on here. People think they're getting close, Rete realizes, but they're really not. They are thinking, "That girl's cool," Rete imagines. Sadly she adds, "They have no idea who I really am."

Her Steps

Rete, at 36, entered **therapy** for the first time. For a woman who trusts no one and despises being vulnerable, this was a major undertaking. Clearly her pain was intolerable and she was wise enough and educated enough to know that if she could have solved these old issues by herself, she would have.

Throughout the years Rete had tried **medicine**, prescribed always by her OB/GYN, but always just anti-depressants, never anything for anxiety. She's been on Zoloft and Lexapro, both of which have an anti-anxiety component. Both had helped, but neither alone, as the research typically confirms, had been enough.

◇◇

PTSD, anxiety and depression are most effectively treated by a combination of medication and therapy.
Neither therapy nor medication alone is as effective as therapy and medication together.

◇◇

Rete had found **movement and exercise** to be incredibly helpful in getting the anxiety out of her body. Unfortunately, as we've discussed, her exercise bordered on and frequently crossed over into self-abuse. So much exercise was needed to battle the mounting tension that Rete was frequently self-mutilating with her exercise and her scalp-picking.

Self-abuse, as we talked about when we talked about Dora early in the book, is a desperate but creative way to calm anxiety. Because anxiety builds in our bodies as we wait and wait for the abuse, sometimes, sadly, only some form of self-abuse can flip us into the "relief" portion of the process. (**Awareness** of what we're doing is the turning point. Once we realize that we are hurting ourselves to makes ourselves feel better, we are almost always freed from that unconscious behavior. Once we're aware of it, we're aware we have other choices, too.)Remember the cycle:

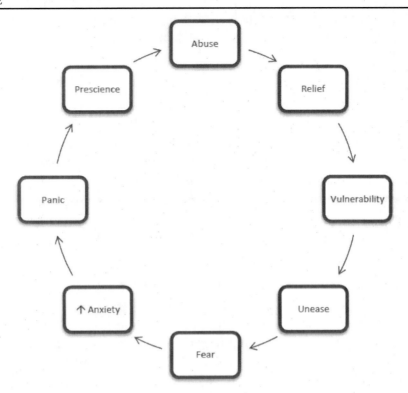

Rete **created a safe place for herself**. She created a home and a family where she could be completely herself. Ben and the kids know her well: her rants, her humors, her generosities, her unrelenting demand of honesty and responsibility, her expectations, her protection of them, her delight in them. They know her and they love her. She is increasingly safe and open and relaxed in her own home.

Rete **protects herself from attacks**. She maintains an unparalleled strength of body and spirit. She tries to live her life with kindness and consideration for others but with no expectations. She doesn't need anyone's approval, she says. As long as she is doing her jobs to her own specifications, she is impervious to criticism. She doesn't engage with people in any way which encourages their feedback. These are ways she keeps herself from attack, she says.

Most of her lifelong criticism, of course, has come from her parents, and Rete has worked hard to **establish healthy boundaries** with her mother. When her mother calls on the phone, Rete only answers if she has her armor on. She told me about one time when one of the kid's pets had died and her mom was trying to call her but Rete was trying to help her child with grief and feeling vulnerable herself, so she simply didn't answer. She now frequently goes to exercise after she has been on the phone with her mother. She says she has to get the toxicity right on out of her body.

Rete has also come to the end of the road of hope with her mother. She no longer hopes and believes, when her mother has been kind for days or weeks at a time, that this time it'll be different. She says she has a cold certainty inside herself now that she will never get any "mothering" from her own mother. It makes her more determined than ever to give it to her children. Rete **expects nothing helpful or healthy to come to her from her mother**. She has decided, though, that she owes her mother courtesy and respect. She walks the balance beam of giving her mother what she would give any stranger and expecting nothing more from her mother than she might expect from a stranger.

Rete **understands the mind/body connection**. She has come to understand that when she can keep her body free of tension, she helps herself to stay free of mental and emotional tension, as well. Anxiety, she realizes, is a full body/mind experience. When her mind feels overwhelmed, she exercises. When her body feels tense, she exercises. Rete has a very clean house, can paint a room in a day, and rarely goes a week without rearranging the furniture in every room. Rete has learned how to move her anxiety right on out of her body/mind.

Rete is at the place where she is able to say, "Anxiety is not a good thing, but I don't see it as necessarily bad, either." She explains: "**Anxiety protects me; I've come to listen to it.**" She says when her heart rate goes up and she has that "high, revved up feeling" and she's "panicky" and is she breathing higher, no longer from her diaphragm but from her throat, and that her chest "feels tight," she needs to pay attention. Her alarm system is going off. Danger is imminent. Armor on. Defenses up. Rete has come to **value her anxiety for the alarm system it is.** She has made friends with her anxiety.

Rete has also come to see that her anxiety often kicks in when it's no longer needed–anytime there is anything uncertain lurking in the shadows. Recently Ben and Rete were trying to make a family decision about some new furniture. In the past, Rete would have raced out and gotten the furniture just to have the decision made. She **understands now that she acts impetuously because she's trying to avoid the limbo that arrives with any uncertainty.** Anytime there's a decision hanging in the air, she wants it solved as quickly as possible. The limbo is unbearable because for Rete it comes complete with anxiety. She is very proud of herself this time. She's thinking about the decision, weighing the pros and cons, consciously choosing to have something that is not completely nailed down and not totally and immediately controlled. This is a time when her anxiety is not necessarily called for. She's **learning when to use her anxiety and when to set it aside.**

My Story

Rete's case study is full of detail, much more so than most of the stories in this book. The detail is a gift from Rete, who knew I was working on a book about anxiety and wanted to help. The details are also a gift from Rete, because she is a social worker and knows the language of psychology.

Her early family life left Rete frozen in speech. She was not permitted to verbalize what she saw and what she felt. Consequently, Rete has a lot of words which need to come out. She has tried journaling and it's too slow for her. She prefers talking, when she has a chance to do so safely. She wants to talk about her anxiety, because she wants to understand it and deal with it in the most helpful ways possible.

Rete is also an exceptionally bright and observant woman. So, I've included as many of her observations as possible in the hopes that she's speaking for many who can't express their pain and frustration so eloquently.

Rete's story is important to us in our understanding of anxiety because Rete is undoubtedly the healthiest looking of the 12 case studies, mentally and emotionally healthy as well as physically healthy. And yet her wounds are incredibly deep and scarring, and her residual anxiety is unlikely ever to dissipate completely. Even those, like Rete, who don't appear to be anxious, can be plagued for life.

Rete won't ever be free of her anxiety. She'll continue to exercise excessively and to keep herself strong and on-guard. But in the time we've worked together, I've seen her come to trust me and this will lead her to trust others, slowly and with caution, but unerringly. Rete will relax into what and who is safe, and her safety net will grow to expand beyond her own home and those who live there with her.

And, if you want someone for your list of who to take to your desert island or who to choose for your dream team: grab Rete. She's your girl for protection. If you're a good person, she can sense it and will fight to the death for you. And if you have Rete on your team, you'll have moral and physical strength. She has used a truly difficult childhood as a template of who not to be and what not to value. She has used her upbringing to transform herself into a woman of power. And she is accomplishing that one most admirable thing: she is refusing to pass on to her children what was passed to her and is making different, healthier, happier choices. The buck stopped with Rete.

AMANDA

Her Story

Amanda started crying when she sat down and I said, "Hello." Her intake sheet had said, "anxiety." Apparently her anxiety was no longer going to be managed by her previous methods. "I think I need some help," she admitted.

"Okay," I suggested, as I always do, "Let's start with a genogram of your family of origin and the family you're a part of now." This is the way I begin every first therapy session. The research I saw on genograms 25 years ago suggested that beginning with that collection of data saved six sessions of therapy. I don't know if that's still the statistic. What I do know is that starting a therapeutic relationship by completing a genogram allows me to hit the ground running. Also, since I'm a visual learner, drawing a picture and actually seeing someone's family on paper greatly aids my ability to remember names and relationship details.

A genogram is a picture. The women are represented by circles and the men are represented by squares. (Hey, I didn't make this up!). So we might have:

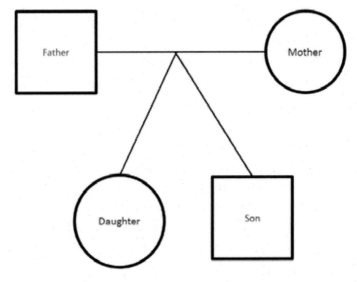

Then we might add ages and some pertinent details:

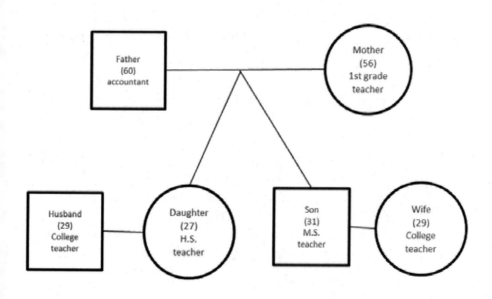

We're already starting to get a feel for this family. Now we might start adding grandparents, aunts, uncles, and children, as well as psychological or behavioral details, like this child has ADHD and this uncle is an alcoholic. If family members are deceased, we put an X through them, recording when they died and from what.

I did a genogram of a new client last week and at least half the folks on the page were alcoholics or drug addicts, including an alcoholic mom and an alcoholic dad. Dad had sexually abused my client and Mom had been unable to protect him. First ten minutes of the first session and we're in the heart of the matter. And I couldn't begin to count the number of times when I've asked a client to tell me about his or her mom and the answer has been, "Well, that's probably why I'm here."

But Amanda's genogram wasn't immediately revealing of any family dysfunction. Mom was loving and kind, dad had died of a massive heart attack in his 50's. The grandparents were all gone, but had all been good grandparents and good people, and Amanda had one younger sister who was happily married with two small children.

Amanda was recently divorced, but she believed she and her ex-husband were doing a good job of co-parenting. Who had initiated the divorce, I wondered out loud? Well, she reluctantly said, she had.

It seems Amanda, a nurse in a doctor's office, had fallen in love with the doctor. The doctor had fallen in love with her, too. Amanda is already divorced and the doctor is in the process of divorcing. His wife is not being as cooperative as Amanda's husband.

Ah, I think. Here we are. This is the issue. Not only is she the first person on either side of her family to divorce, but look at the circumstances. She has been raised with strong moral values about marriage. Now she not only divorces, but initiates the divorce, to leave her marriage for another man, breaking up two families. And it is apparently common knowledge in their small community that they are having an affair. She feels like the scarlet woman. Well, that's enough to make anyone anxious.

So we spent our first few sessions talking about guilt, self-forgiveness, freeing ourselves from the effects of gossip, etc. I asked her how her anxiety was. "Well," she answered, "I'm still throwing up." (Talk about an unexpected answer!)

It turns out that Amanda, slim, trim, tennis-playing Amanda, who exercises religiously and is in great physical condition, has been bulimic for her entire adult life. This is a secret that only her doctor/significant other knows. Her mom and sister don't know, her three children have never caught her, her ex-husband was clueless, and even her closest friends have no idea.

Bulimia, of course, is a symptom, not a disease. What causes someone to start throwing up and then to continue throwing up, sticking her fingers down her own throat to keep from ingesting calories?

Amanda was able to pinpoint the start of the bulimia to her nineteenth year. She was in college on a tennis scholarship, getting a BS/RN degree and eating dorm food. I asked her what else happened when she was 19? Her dad died.

Her dad had been her tennis coach, her athletic trainer and her best cheerleader. He had also kept an eagle eye on her weight and monitored what she ate, how much, when, what she drank, when she exercised, how she cross-trained and how much she slept. He had total control of Amanda's routine and regimen. A perfectionist himself, he made sure she did everything perfectly.

Her Signs

Amanda *looked perfect*. Her hair was perfect, her make-up was perfect, her clothes were perfect, her body was toned and slim and muscular and agile. Amanda, in fact, looked too perfect.

She *exercised extensively and intensely* five mornings a week before she got the kids up. She washed and styled her long hair every morning. Then she spent about a half hour, she guessed, on her make-up. Next, she ironed her scrubs for the day. Finally, it was time to awaken the three kids and get them fed, dressed and organized so they could catch the bus to school and she could get to the medical office.

She always *arrived at work early and stayed at work late*. Her charting was always completely finished before she went home for the day, and her examining rooms were spotless and stocked for the next day. Amanda never ran out of supplies and was excellent in emergencies. Amanda was always prepared, re-prepared, completely prepared and over-prepared.

All the doctor's patients adored and asked for Amanda. She spent as long as it took with each and every one of them. She made sure that when they left the office they knew exactly what was going on with them and that they were completely satisfied with their care. Amanda was also the angel of follow-up calls.

Her *need to be perfect*, as her dad had so carefully taught her, was exhausting her and crippling her. Amanda's perfectionism had played a big part in the demise of her first marriage, and, she suspected, was one reason her ex-husband was so cooperative about the divorce. He was relieved. He hadn't been able to meet her standards and keep up with her demands for perfection. He wasn't perfect and had no desire to be perfect.

Amanda's *bulimia* was the most debilitating sign of her anxiety. *Her teeth and skin were suffering* from her self-abuse and *she was exhausted* not only from the physical torment of making herself vomit every day, but even more so from the mental and emotional torment. Amanda was dying from the weight of *her secret* and from *her shame* that she was behaving in such a sick way. In all of her adult life, unless she was pregnant, she had never gone more than five consecutive days without purging.

Amanda *counted calories and deprived herself of any pleasure from food or beverages*. She wouldn't allow herself to drink anything except water. If she was meeting friends at a bar or restaurant, she would limit herself to one glass of red wine and a side salad with no dressing. *Food was her enemy*. Anything she ate, she either had to exercise away or purge out. She was actually proud of herself that she had never used laxatives.

Amanda felt incredible *guilt* about breaking up two marriages. She told me that her new lover felt horrible guilt also, but it was obvious to me that she was in therapy alone.

Amanda had tried every trick in the book to stop purging. She ate only healthful things and ate so little that she couldn't possibly gain weight. But every few days she would break down and eat something she shouldn't have, like cheese and crackers or a pretzel. She rarely allowed herself meat, and then, only chicken, and she never ate sweets. No matter how careful she was or how much she deprived herself, she was *rarely able to convince herself that she didn't need to throw up* that day.

She reported feeling "relieved" after she vomited. She was "safe" and wouldn't "get fat," she said. Her body unfortunately was taking a beating, even as her mind tried to tell her how well she was doing. She was *constantly constipated and bloated*. She frequently had *stomach cramps*. She *rarely had periods*. She *couldn't enjoy sex*. Sex hurt her skin, especially her vaginal walls, which were very thin and dry. She apparently had none of the oils that lubricate the vaginal area. Also, her *hormones were out of whack*, and so *her libido, as well, was compromised*.

Her Steps

Amanda was in her mid-thirties when she **entered therapy** for the first time. I think the fact that she focused on things other than the bulimia for a few sessions helped her get used to the idea of therapy. She was able to be comfortable with me and the knowledge that judgment was not a part of the therapeutic process. She got to settle in a little before she had to **tell the big secret**.

We worked on **self-awareness, self-acceptance and self-forgiveness** around issues other than the one about which she felt such shame. We formed a bond and learned to work together.

Amanda was, of course, a perfect client. She tried everything I suggested. First, she **started journaling**. Once she was getting some of her old thinking out of her body, she **started reading**. I suggested Clarissa Pinkola Estes and Pema Chodron to help Amanda with the battle for mature self-acceptance and some lessening of the tight control under which she always held herself.

We **talked a great deal about her dad**. Together we helped him down off his pedestal and worked toward a much more realistic view of him. He had abused her mentally and physically with his incessant demands for perfection. His similar demands on himself had no doubt led to his Type A personality and that his driven personality had no doubt contributed to his massive coronary.

We talked about how innocent and healthy his intentions may have been, but that the way he brought those intentions to fruition had harmed her terribly and insidiously. The better athlete she became, the more he expected and demanded. The more he expected and demanded, the more she excelled. Together they created a destructive, negative feedback loop that may have helped kill him and that would surely kill her if she didn't make some significant changes.

We **looked at her parenting of her own children** and tried to separate out any of her own innocent intentions which might be leading to harmful results. She was a beautiful woman and a strong, natural athlete. Her children didn't need to achieve such extreme results to be happy or successful. She was able to pinpoint signs of anxiety in all three of the children, but in the oldest, especially. We got that child into therapy immediately.

Amanda had vehemently refused the idea of anti-anxiety or anti-depression medication. She knew that most anti-depressants had weight gain as a side effect. She knew herself well enough to know that weight gain, no matter how much better she felt on the medication, would be a deal-breaker.

Recently one of my clients had found **an all natural anti-anxiety medication** called Theanine Serene with Relora which was available in health food stores and had no weight gain side effect. The client had told me she simply "felt better" on the Theanine, less stressed, less critical of self and others, and more able to roll with the punches. I wrote down the name of the supplement for Amanda and suggested she look it up. She might choose to use that if she thought it might be good for her.

Amanda immediately did her research and started the Theanine. After a few days, she was able to talk herself out of purging. I saw her after about seven days of no bulimic activity, and we were both ecstatic. I predicted an imperfect path out of this bulimic quicksand, told her she would revert to the bulimia, and she needed to be prepared for the inevitable relapse. It didn't mean she couldn't stop purging. It did mean she couldn't completely stop the first time she tried. She wasn't perfect! (Anymore.)

I also asked her to **see a nutritionist** and get a consultation on how to eat healthfully without weight gain. Amanda and I thought a dietician or nutritionist might be able to suggest ways to repair some teeth, skin, and intestinal damage that her years of bulimia had caused. Neither Amanda nor I knew if she would be strong enough to share the shameful secret and ask the necessary questions.

I had been seeing Amanda every other week at this point, and after this visit Amanda cancelled two appointments. We went six weeks without seeing each other. I thought this was a bad indicator, and I expected we would have to face a pretty big set-back.

Amanda sat down and smiled at me. "43 days," she said. I cried that time. She went **43 days without throwing up**, and then her anxiety got the best of her and she purged, and then she went back to not purging. She was ready for the "oops" and she didn't let it derail her. **She no longer needed to be perfect**. And she certainly didn't need to be perfect to get better.

My Story

"Trust the timing," is one of the phrases I use frequently in therapy and it sums up the incredible good fortune in this case. A client of mine had just come in telling me about this herbal, all-natural anti-anxiety "stuff" she found. She thought it was helping her relax and go with the flow. On a scale of 1 to 10, with 1 being no change and 10 being all the difference in the world, the client who found the Theanine probably would have given it about a 3 in her life. I passed the information on to Amanda, doubting she'd ever try it, and she not only tried it, but those natural herbs were just the push she needed to be able to break a horrific, harmful addiction, which all too easily could have become fatal. Instead, Amanda got her life back. Trust the timing.

◇◇

TRUST THE TIMING

◇◇

Another saying I use often is, "Just plant the seeds." We never know, in many cases, which seeds will grow, which will fall fallow, and which will be eaten by the birds and squirrels before they even germinate. It doesn't matter. As therapists and parents and friends and teachers and lovers, we just need to keep planting the seeds.

◇◇

PLANT THE SEEDS

◇◇

We don't get very many quick fixes in therapy. What we more often get is pieces of a long, arduous process. But Amanda was able to stop purging, she started having periods again, her constipation and bloating became rare instead of constant, and she is working with her oldest child to stop the perfectionism that has been passed down in her family for generations. That child will have help with perfectionism before the perfectionism grows into a destructive, shameful blob that needs to be purged routinely from her body.

Years ago a perfectionistic client was able to off-load a heavy portion of her perfectionism. She felt grateful, although she did the work, and she made me a present. It's a beautiful cross-stitched picture of a group of baby bears playing with blocks and it says, "Therapists help make life bearable." I love the metaphor of the blocks as the building blocks which therapy tries to provide. The picture is matted and framed professionally, and it hangs in my office where clients can see it. But the best part of the present is that there is a mistake in the stitching. There's a missing stitch. It's a small error, and no one would ever notice it. But no perfectionist could ever take such a piece to a framer and then give it as a present. "See how far I've come," she crowed, as she gave it to me. She didn't have to be perfect anymore.

There's a saying in psychology: Would you rather be right or be happy? You can't be both. If you need to be right, you'll never be happy. If you need to be perfect, you'll never be happy, either. The Amish put a mistake in every quilt they sew because only God is perfect. Here's to imperfection. It's so healthy.

Think of the medical example of a child who grows up in a perfect, sterile environment. That child never gets to develop immunities. Flu shots, measles shots, etc., are little bits of the virus injected into our bodies. Those little bits of toxin protect us from getting the whole, dreaded disease.

Small mistakes, small errors. small mishaps are all protective as well. Imperfection is protective and healthy. A little dirt, a few germs, a misspoken word a, mismatched outfit – they keep us healthy and humble.

◇◇◇

GOD GRANT US THE FREEDOM
TO BE IMPERFECT
THAT WE MAY LIVE
WITHOUT (too much) ANXIETY

◇◇◇

One more footnote on Amanda and her unusually quick results from therapy. Amanda, like Carrie, the rape survivor in The Many Faces of

PTSD, had a supportive, protective childhood. When we have childhoods (especially the first five years) in which we are allowed to be children, given age-appropriate challenges, allowed to stumble and pick ourselves back up, when we're protected but not smothered, when we're loved and encouraged and teased and taught and disciplined and delighted in, then we grow up with resiliency. Resiliency is that invisible quality we begin to possess as children, if we are parented in a healthy way. When we grow up with resiliency, we can come back from difficulties. We have learned and hold in our bone marrow the knowledge that we are enough, that we have enough, that enough will be provided. Enough. Not everything. But enough.

Amanda and Carrie had "happy" childhoods and, because they did, they were prepared for adversity in adulthood. They could meet adversity and not be taken down by it, whether it came in the disguise of bulimia or rape or divorce or disease or anything else. Adversity can be overcome in adult years whether we had happy childhoods or not. It's just easier and quicker if you happened to luck out and get healthy parents.

BECKY

Her Story

Becky came into individual therapy, referred by a fellow counselor who was working with Becky and her husband in marital therapy. She needed help with her "anger." When I met her, it was not the first time I had met someone purported to be "angry" who seemed anything but. Becky was calm, sweet, friendly, very bright and quite articulate. The explanation of her angry reputation became my first hypothesis: Becky is not an angry person, she is a person who is angry at and about something specific, in this case, her husband.

Becky was 40, had been married for 20 years, and had no children. And now she was furious with her husband. For the long years of their marriage, she had learned to care for herself when she felt vulnerable and unprotected. Jack was useless at emotion.

Becky's mom was critical and controlling. Her dad was passive and interested only in pacifying her mom. He was the consummate peace-keeper and ass-kisser. Whatever would calm mom's troubled rages was what he made happen. Unfortunately, for Becky, the rages were usually at her, meaning that her mom was constantly mad at her, and her dad thought her mom was always justified and correct, no matter what the issue.

Becky had an older sister and a younger brother. She remembered she and her sister running away from home when they were in elementary school. They grew up overseas, with no extended family and a community culture that changed every few years as they moved from Brazil to Germany to Japan.

Becky's older sister died in a car accident when she was 17. Obviously they were all devastated, but Becky's mom slid into a deep and ugly depression. Becky's dad worked longer and longer hours. Becky's younger brother began contracting illnesses and syndromes. And Becky, at 14, learned to trust no one and to care for herself. She became private, guarded, tense and anxious.

She focused on working hard in school and getting good grades. She learned to make no waves. And she learned that if she became vigilant and observant and hyper-alert at home, she could avoid some of the trouble and limit the amount of time she was the whipping girl for her mother's raging depression. In other words, Becky learned to use anxiety as a self-defense and a coping mechanism.

After graduating from high school Becky came back to the United States and began a lonely existence both at home and at school. Since she had to work her way through college, she had no time for friends or fun. She became an accountant for the IRS, an isolating and isolated profession. She bought a house and before long met Jack, a fellow accountant.

Jack was the strong, silent type. These two accountants kept their home and everything in it in absolute order. It was clean and sterile. This was the way Jack's childhood home had been, and this was the way Jack wanted it.

Jack, like Becky, grew up with a critical mother and a passive, pacifying father.

His father had died from colon cancer on the day he had turned 50. Jack's mom depended on Jack for everything from that day on. Jack had an older sister who had left town to go to college and never come back. After that, she was the black sheep and Jack was the golden child.

When push came to shove and Jack had to decide between doing what his mother wanted and what Becky needed, Becky always lost. Jack was a mama's boy. He stopped by her house every Tuesday and had supper with her, just the two of them. Becky wasn't invited. Then he set out her trash for her before he went home. Mondays he had his bowling league, or golf, depending on the season. Wednesdays he went to the gym. Thursdays he took his mom out to dinner, just the two of them. Fridays he went out for drinks with the guys from work. Weekends he caught up on his sleep, went to the gym, watched porn, shoveled his mom's walks or mowed her grass, again, depending on the season, and without fail took Becky out for dinner every Saturday night.

This had been Jack's schedule for the 20 years of their marriage. There used to be some sex scheduled in there, but that had slowed down about year eight of their marriage and stopped completely by year 14.

At first, Becky accepted Jack's separate life. After all, he told her, he married her because she was so independent. He admired that. She didn't need him. She wasn't one of those weak, clingy women.

So, Becky filled her life with animals. The animals, rescues mostly, gave her warmth and affection and joy. She started with dogs, but because she and Jack had some land and she wasn't afraid of hard work, before long she had chickens and goats and then, finally, horses.

And, so, it seemed, they had achieved their peace. She took care of her rescues, and, indeed, Jack seemed to be one of them. It was Becky who cleaned and paid the bills and mowed *their* lawn and shoveled *their* snow while she worked her full-time job. Jack did the grocery shopping and cooked a big Sunday dinner. It fit in his schedule.

And then things started to change, or, at least, Becky started noticing some changes. He wasn't coming home until hours after the golf or bowling used to end. He stayed in the gym longer and longer. His computer e-mail account started requiring a password as did the e-mail on his phone. He watched more pornography, more blatantly, while giving Becky less and less attention and no affection. Becky started a slow simmer.

These changes might have begun, she supposed, around year 17 of their marriage. But it wasn't until year 20 that American Express called the house to ask some questions about Jack's bill. Becky was about to say that Jack didn't have an American Express card. After all, she paid the bills, and she knew what they had and what they didn't. Then she thought better of it and simply said, "I'll give him the message."

And she did. But, first, she gathered some information. She hacked into his computer and his phone account and discovered not only an American Express account but also one for Victoria's Secret and a separate Visa account. Well. She just *thought* she paid all the bills. And where was he getting this money? Ah-hah. The company hadn't stopped giving bonuses after all. There in his own private bank account were deposits of $10,000 and $20,000 and more. She printed everything off, wrote everything down and congratulated herself that she was such a good little detective.

But, what really made Becky mad was the trail of e-mails that had started with his E-Harmony account and continued on, coming to focus on one person. About six months ago Jack apparently fell in love. It was someone named Missy. Missy? Missy? She wracked her brain. Then, in a moment of clarity, she realized that were it not for the fluke phone call from American Express, she would have gone to see Missy the very next day. Missy was the woman who cut both her hair and Jack's. Becky would have sat in a chair in front of her husband's mistress who would have been holding a scissors and a razor. Now, that didn't seem like a good idea.

Planner that she was, Becky still kept her mouth shut and immediately found a lawyer. "Oh, this guy is dead in the water," is what the lawyer said when Becky showed him her well documented paper trail.

Her Signs

Becky's *anger* was the marriage therapist's indicator of a high level of *anxiety*. Becky's anxiety was easy to track back to her childhood, where life was never safe or predictable. I pointed this out to Becky, especially wondering about their time in the Mid-east, where bombs were an every day occurrence. "Oh," said Becky, "the fireworks outside were nothing compared to the fireworks inside."

Becky's parents fought constantly. Her mom would criticize and condemn and censure not only the children, but her husband, too. He would take it and take it and take it, and then he would lash back. That usually involved physical violence. Then her dad would apologize and bring home presents. Becky remembered that often her parents would then leave on an unplanned trip, just the two of them. Some babysitter or other would be found for the kids, while mom was rewarded for her rages with a vacation. Upon the parents' return, the cycle would start over.

Becky remembers her dad calling the kids together more than once to tell them they had to be better behaved, or mommy might be forced to do something stupid. Becky recognized the blame and manipulation after we talked about it. But as a child, all she knew was that *she was responsible for the well-being of everyone she knew.*

When Becky's sister died, it was explained that it was the fight that Becky and her sister had had that afternoon over a blouse that had no doubt forced her sister to sneak out of the house that night and go to a party which involved alcohol and then get in that car in which she'd been killed. *Becky took on the responsibility of her sister's death.*

Becky *never argued.* That was one thing that made her anger so frightening. She, like her dad, swallowed it and swallowed it until *the white rage broke through.* Becky had no violence in her soul, so there were never physical altercations, but, boy, did she know some words. She took it like her father, but when she reached her saturation point, it came flooding out just like her mother's white rage did.

Becky, like so many other people with anxiety, was a *perfectionist.* I have a difficult time getting most people to keep a journal. Not Becky. She wrote page after page in her neat and perfect handwriting and even devised a code for the margins: "D" for dreams she recorded, "I" for insights she got from the writing, and "S" for the things she wanted to share with Susan, her therapist. Her hair, no longer cut and styled by Missy, was always perfect, as was her slender figure, as was her clothing. She was early for every appointment and totally in charge of her life. In fact, to be truthful, Becky was a *control freak*. I had never seen anything as meticulous as her planner.

Being controlling, of course, makes complete sense for someone who is plagued by anxiety. Anxiety is fear of the future and fear of the unknown. The more we can control that unknown future, the more we can reduce our own anxiety. Anxiety practically predicts control.

><><><><><><><><><><><><><><><><><><><><><><><><><><><><><><><><><

Anxiety is fear of the future.
Anxiety is fear of the unknown.
The more we can control our future and the unknown,
the more we can reduce our anxiety.
Someone who is controlling suffers from anxiety.
No exceptions.

><><><><><><><><><><><><><><><><><><><><><><><><><><><><><><><><><

Becky was a *planner* and a *doer*. She was a "J" on the Myers/Briggs. She knew where she was going to be three weeks from Tuesday at 10 a.m. Becky was *unfailingly reliable, responsible* and *loyal*. Jack launched her into action when he betrayed her and disrespected her loyalty.

Her Steps

Becky had started **working on her marriage** years before they entered marital therapy. One of Becky's first steps was to **befriend her mother-in-law.** She started calling her to say hello and inviting her over when Jack was cooking something good. When they had Becky's family for a holiday, Becky invited her mother-in-law, too. Becky took her to lunch and bought her presents if she saw something she thought her mother-in-law would like. They never became friends, but they became comfortable acquaintances, and I told Becky how much I admired that effort. "Well," she said, "Jack always used to tell me what a horrible person I was to be jealous of his mother, so I thought I'd get that issue out of the way."

><><><><><><><><><><><><><><><><><><><><><><><><><><><><><><><><><

Keep your friends close,
and your enemies (and mother-in-law) closer.

><><><><><><><><><><><><><><><><><><><><><><><><><><><><><><><><><

Becky found **Retrouvaille** and convinced Jack to give it a try. Retrouvaille is a Catholic program which accepts couples from all faiths as well as those without a declared faith, in fact, any couple who want a "lifeline" for their marriage. Retrouvaille brings people together on weekends and offers information and ideas for reviving relationships and rededicating to them. I have two couples, clients, who have attended. Both had good things to say about the program.

Becky reported that immediately after they attended Retrouvaille things did improve in their marriage. They wrote in their journals and read to each other what they wrote. Becky said she got out a lot of anger and resentment. It was only in the year after this that Becky realized she was always the one to say, "Let's write," or "Let's talk," or "Let's go on a date." Finally she got fed up with the one-way-street and went back to her slow simmer.

When Becky traced back the timing, she realized that Jack had been on the dating site, e-mailing other women and spending money at Victoria's Secret, the entire time she was dragging him to Retrouvaille and working to enrich their marriage. No wonder she was simmering.

Before coming into **individual therapy**, Becky had worked on herself in order to improve her marriage. Now **Becky refocused her therapy work on herself. She wanted to improve herself, not her marriage.** We explored her childhood and found the roots of early and pervasive anxiety. As with most people, when I mentioned the word *anxiety*, she didn't think it applied to her. Finally, **she realized a number of things about herself.** She was anxious, as well as controlling, hyper-vigilant and fearful. She was afraid of missing a deadline or presenting a fact incorrectly, and she checked and double-checked herself until she drove herself nearly batty.

Also, like many controlling perfectionists with anxiety, Becky was a pack-rat. She didn't quite approach the level of a hoarder, but her anxiety demanded that she hold on to every pet supply, tool, empty bucket, dug up rock, paper and magazine. She was afraid to throw anything away for fear she'd find out, sometime in that unknown future, that she needed just what she'd tossed.

Awareness of what she was doing and why made a big difference for Becky.

She laughed that she could probably find other rocks and empty buckets. And, when prodded, she agreed that in the days of the Internet, hanging onto paper copies of things is really unnecessary. (I, for example, as a former speech teacher, had a filing cabinet drawer full of speeches: Martin Luther King, Jr's "I Have A Dream" speech and inaugural addresses by Lincoln and Kennedy and a whole mass of other speeches from which I might have needed a reference. Gone. I can find it on the Internet more quickly than I can walk to the back bedroom where the filing cabinet is and go through the drawer.)

The Artist's Way by Julia Cameron made a big impact in Becky's life. Reading this book helped Becky learn to slow down and play by herself. With her job and her farm full of animals, Becky didn't have much spare time. The idea from the book of "an artist's date" with oneself became a very helpful anxiety-reducing tool for Becky. And she could schedule it – her favorite thing.

Pilate's class was another way Becky discovered to calm her anxiety and release some of that tension. It is always true that body tension creates tension in our minds and hearts, and tension in our minds and hearts translates to stiff, brittle bodies. Reducing any tension reduces all tension.

◇◇◇

The mind/body connection is especially strong for anxiety and tension.
Many anxious people find exercise to be a great anti-anxiety tool.
Something like yoga, which exercises the body and the mind, is perfect. But any exercise reduces tension. Moving reduces tension.

◇◇◇

Pilates also gave Becky a chance to **make some new friends**. She began to **volunteer**, and that, also, was an opportunity to make friends and build self-esteem.

As with all working clients, I suggested to Becky what my friend Jim Moffitt calls "the trickle-down theory of the economy." If you're working full-time making money, spend some of it employing others. Hire a cleaning person, a landscaper, a dog-walker, or a personal chef. Make your own life more sane while financially aiding someone else. Becky hated cleaning. Most packrats do. It's too overwhelming. So, she **hired a cleaning person** and found that things were much easier to keep neat and tidy when the toilets and floors and windows were already sparkling.

Becky **went on an anti-depressant** for a while, and what we discovered was that she has SAD, Seasonal Affective Disorder. This is, for her, exacerbated by how active she is and how much she loves the outdoors. Here in Ohio it is difficult to be active enough and find sunshine enough October through April. Now Becky goes on her anti-depressant every September and starts weaning off it every April. When she can get outside and work outside and enjoy nature, her depression lifts and her anxiety is reduced. When she can't, she leans on her anti-depressant for help.

Becky **divorced** quickly and well. Indeed, her husband was "dead in the water," as her attorney had predicted. Because a great deal of the money he had secreted away was half hers, Becky decided to **start working half-time** instead of full-time, which also greatly reduced her anxiety and allowed her more time for care of herself and the occupants of the barn.

My Story

Becky stayed in therapy for about five years after her divorce. She had a lot to learn about what had landed her in her situation and she was bright enough and eager enough to want to learn it. She wanted to study her past so as not to be a victim of repeating it in her future.

Becky's parents had set her up for anxiety. Her childhood was not predictable in any way, starting with the frequent moves and changes in culture. Living in Germany is a very different experience from living in Brazil or Lebanon. As a child, one has a lot of resiliency, but it is downright confusing when one no sooner learns Spanish then everyone on the street is speaking German. This uncertainty and cultural chaos really requires a stable family life for balance. Becky didn't have that.

Becky's parents had obviously come to their parenting with some awful examples of parenting in their own lives. Neither Becky's mom nor dad had the ego strength to put their children's needs first. Consequently, Becky was made to bear the weight of their anxiety and depression and guilt and self-hatred. Who blames a child for a car accident that simply happens a few hours after two sisters have a fight? Becky had only a few examples like this, although they were powerful examples. Having been a therapist for 25 years now, I know this: for everything we remember, good, bad or indifferent, there were a hundred other similar events. Becky was raised to be the scapegoat.

So, when Jack said things like, "What kind of woman are you to be jealous of my mother," or "What kind of wife would resent her husband for going to the gym so he can stay healthy," he shut her right down. Obviously something was wrong with her. She was to blame. She was the scapegoat.

Becky and I had the twin benefits of hindsight and proof when it came to Jack. It was easy from such a vantage point to see his manipulative traps and the way she fell into them. She learned to go into her head and analyze things for which she was blamed. She still had plenty of on-going examples from her mother and one of her bosses. She would sit on the accusations with the acknowledgment that she'd "think about it." At first we had to talk about examples one by one, but Becky quickly became adept at sorting out what was her responsibility and what was under her control and what wasn't.

Becky's mom was also an on-going study in guilt, and so Becky and I worked on when we should bear guilt (almost never) and what to do with it when it's thrown at us, which is to set it back, politely, at the feet of the person who tossed it at us in the first place.

Here's a brief example. See if you can picture this:

Mom throws (a ball of) guilt at Becky, Becky catches it and calmly sets it down on the ground at her mother's feet.

Mom: "You haven't called for two weeks."

Becky: (Puts the ball down on the ground. She's not playing and she's not going to defend herself) "Nope. Was there something you wanted?"

Mom: "Well, yes, I'd like my daughter to show some respect."

Becky: (Puts that ball down on the ground by ignoring it completely) "How's dad?"

Mom: "Are you changing the subject?"

Becky: "Yes. How is he?"

Mom: sighs and gives up. This guilt stuff isn't working. "Well, he . . . ."

Becky has designed a new life for herself. She has made new friends, found new interests, worked hard to rid herself of guilt and shame and blame and does things she loves to keep the tension out of her body and her mind. If you ask her if she's happy, she'll tell you she absolutely is. She's even doing something which is totally imperfect:

She's living with a man who is separated from his wife but cannot get her to agree to a divorce. So, rather than wait for the perfect circumstances, they went ahead and are living together and loving each other. Imperfectly.

VIRGINIA

Her Story

Virginia is a striking woman, tall, statuesque and muscular, with jet black hair and soft black eyes. When we met, her face was lined with tension, and she looked beaten.

We started with a genogram. Virginia's family owns a successful dry cleaning business with half a dozen different stores. Her dad supposedly runs the business, but, actually, her mom controls how everything and everyone functions. Virginia's parents have been married over 40 years. They have lived apart for most of that time, but there has never been so much as a whisper about divorce. Her parents can meet for occasions and holidays, but they can't live together. In fact, Virginia offers hesitantly, no one can live with her mother.

Virginia's mother is a perfectionist and "a hard task master." There is a great deal of turnover in the help at the stores, because Virginia's mom likes to pop in and check up on things. Her dad hires them, and her mom fires them.

Virginia and her sisters have all worked for the business. Her oldest sister is now exempt from "doing her part," since she is married and the mother of the only grandchild. Her next sister does all the payroll for the business. She's single. Virginia's younger brother, also single, is career military and travels the world. There's a ticker-tape parade any time he comes to town. There are, after all, four children, but only one son.

Virginia graduated from college with a business degree, but business was not her passion. She went through college with a "free ride" to play women's softball. She turned pro immediately after graduation. Softball was her love and her life. At least it was until her body decided otherwise. Virginia collapsed on the field during a tense game with her first attack of Crohn's disease. She spent the next six months in the hospital and then her mom's house resting and recuperating. Her athletic career was over.

Virginia now works for a non-profit. She loves the work, finds it meaningful, and has lots of flexibility in her schedule, which she needs. Crohn's doesn't obey a schedule and doesn't go away. Virginia has had eight serious bouts with the disease and three major surgeries. Her life has become one on-going attempt to function normally while being constantly alert to the horrors of stomach cramps, diarrhea, accidents and humiliation. Needless to say, Virginia suffers from anxiety.

Virginia's mom was a devout Catholic. She went to mass every day and did more for the priest in terms of cooking and cleaning and care than she ever did for her husband. The kids all joked about the role of "the father" in their lives. Mary Alice, the second sibling, accompanied her mother to mass and joined her in her devotion to Catholicism.

Anne Marie, the oldest sibling, married the son of an Episcopal priest, and so Anne Marie fled to the Episcopalians. John Paul, the youngest sibling, despite being named for a pope, is, Virginia says, "non-religious." Virginia is very active in a charismatic religious group called The New Vine. That's where she met her husband, Russ.

Their union is Russ' second marriage and Virginia's first. They've been married six years. The marriage is unconsummated. Virginia is terrified of sex. She was sexually molested by an older neighbor when she was about eight. She never told anyone until she told me during our first therapy session.

My reaction to such news is always the same, straight from my mother-heart: "I am so sorry. That should not have happened. You should not have had to endure that, then or in all the years since. I am so dreadfully sorry." Protecting our children is clearly the number one job of every mother on earth. When this fundamental right of every child, to be protected, is not granted, for whatever reason, it absolutely breaks my heart, and I have no trouble at all saying that I am so dreadfully sorry. If you, who are reading this now, weren't protected, I am so dreadfully sorry.

It is the fundamental right of every child to be protected by his or her parents.
It is the fundamental duty of every parent to protect his or her child.
If you are reading this book at this moment and you were not protected:
Please feel my sorrow. I have worked with too many survivors who have never heard those words: I am so sorry.
Many voices join mine in saying to you now: we are so sorry.
Please forgive us for not protecting you.

Later we talked about what Virginia's husband had to say about the lack of sex in their marriage. He understood, Virginia explained, about the Crohn's and the horrendous body image that often accompanies the disease, and he is content to just wait. "He is trusting God to resolve things for us," Virginia said.

Russ has children from his first marriage, and Russ and Virginia enjoy the kids every other weekend. He likes his job, and he loves his church, and he frequently tells Virginia that he loves her, too, and that he's glad they got married.

She doesn't believe him. She feels unworthy, inadequate, ugly, gross, like a burden and like a terrible wife. She wants to try to learn to endure sex. ("Endure" was the word she used.) In her late 30s, she's never had sex. She has never, in fact, gotten any pleasure from her body. As an athlete, she demanded much from her body and worked it and beat it up. As a Crohn's survivor, her body has demanded much from her. But never have she and her body enjoyed or liked or pleasured each other.

Virginia's dad is a passive man who asks nothing for himself. He doesn't even demand an end to the fraud of being married but living separately and alone. He runs the business, watches sports on television and sleeps in his one bedroom apartment.

Virginia's mom lives in the sprawling, elegant house set on three acres. The inequity of this arrangement apparently suits both of Virginia's parents, since no one makes a move to change things.

Virginia came into therapy, she told me, to learn to deal with her mom. "She's a good person," Virginia hastened to assure me. I'm struck that someone living in a six-year old sexless marriage and suffering from Crohn's prioritizes the relationship with her mother as her biggest problem. This is very telling.

Here is yet another lesson for a therapist. Never, ever, assume "what hurts the most." Always ask.

Assume nothing in therapy.
A client's most pressing issue is not always what one might imagine.
Assume nothing. Always ask.

Her Signs

Virginia has *Crohn's disease.* Crohn's is one of the most debilitating chronic illnesses a person can endure. Crohn's is an inflammatory bowel disease and an auto-immune disorder. What this means is that the immune system mistakenly attacks and destroys healthy body tissue.

For Virginia this means that she has little or no control over bowel movements. She said she'd be rich if she had a dollar for every time she had an "accident" while hurrying to a bathroom or hurrying home. Virginia carries baby wipes and a change of clothes with her wherever she goes. She'll have months with no problems, and then, out of the blue, but usually in a stressful situation, she'll find herself once again unable to make it to the bathroom.

That's the humiliating part of Crohn's for Virginia. Then there's the pain, the bloating, the cramping, the fatigue. She, the indefatigable athlete, is always tired. The three major predictors of Crohn's are family history, being Jewish, and smoking. She has none of these.

What Virginia does have is *anxiety*. She has *debilitating, sleepless, unable-to-calm-down anxiety.* "You know you're in trouble," she tries to joke, "when at 38 you're still worried about pooping your pants." Crohn's as a cause of anxiety would be plenty in and of itself. But Virginia has many more reasons for being anxious and many more signs of her anxiety.

Did Virginia have anxiety before Crohn's? Yes. Absolutely. She remembers the *panic, the hyper-vigilance, the inability to focus, the impulsivity mixed with the inability to make a decision, the insecurity, the feelings of self-loathing, the perfectionism, the inner critic, the sweating and the fear.* But before the Crohn's, Virginia managed her anxiety with *extreme exercise*, the same coping mechanism Rete uses, if you remember her case study. Virginia did her best to exercise the tension right out of her body. Since Crohn's, she has had to sit with the tension, and the anxiety has escalated.

Virginia is unable to enjoy even the most simple pleasures of life. *She can't eat*, for fear of pooping issues. *She can't sleep* because of her anxiety and her tight, critical self-control. *She can't have sex* because, among other things, she can't focus or calm down or let herself go. *She can't enjoy life.*

Virginia has a toxic relationship with her mother. Her mother is a critical slave-driver. Her mother badgers her and finds fault on the one hand, and on the other hand, is overly-doting and enabling. Virginia and her mother have a fear-based relationship. When either is frightened of anything, or has an ailment or a hurt feeling or a worry, the other leaps in and exacerbates it, taking something manageable to its worst possible outcome. If one of them has a headache, the other believes it to be a brain tumor. If one of their names isn't listed in the church bulletin with the volunteers or the donors to something, the whole church is talking about them behind their backs. Nothing is simply what it is. Everything is exaggerated by fear, and fear is the most contagious emotion.

◇◇

Fear is the most contagious emotion.
This led Winston Churchill to say:
"We have nothing to fear but fear itself."

◇◇

Virginia also has *undiagnosed and untreated PTSD*. Being diagnosed as a posttraumatic stress survivor is usually a big relief to people, and Virginia was no exception. Unlike most mental health diagnoses, when you are diagnosed with PTSD, you, the sufferer, are totally innocent. You have been the victim of a trauma, or a series of traumas, and you are simply stuck with the post trauma reactions: hyper-vigilance, lack of trust, anxiety, depression, inability to focus or concentrate, and so forth. All of these symptoms seem much more manageable when we understand why we feel and behave in the ways that we do.

Virginia has *broken and wounded relationships*. When one grows up not being able to trust one's own mother, who, then, really, can one trust? A mother is supposed to protect and defend us. A mother is supposed to nurture and encourage us. A mother is supposed to find the good in us when the rest of the world finds us lacking. Virginia's mother did the exact opposite of all of these basics of mothering.

When our mother betrays us through criticism and condemnation, we are like a young plant devoid of sunshine. We'll never blossom and bloom. Virginia pushed herself through high school and college and then beat herself up for three years as a professional athlete. She was never good enough. She never trained hard enough. If she wasn't the MVP of every game, it wasn't good enough. Her sense of her own self-worth was so diminished, that no amount of external reassurance could fill the emptiness.

Virginia had *no friends*. Wherever she went, she made new acquaintances, but she had no friends. Once again, without trust, friendship can't grow, and when one can't trust one's own mother, how can one trust a stranger to become a friend?

◇◇◇

When you can't trust your own mother,
you will most likely trust no one.

◇◇◇

According to Erikson's stages of psychological growth, trust is something we learn around the age of two. Because we learn trust at such an
early age, we need to be able to trust the mother or the mother figure in
our lives. Learning to trust affects our entire life path and each of our
relationships. It is normal to trust someone until they prove themselves
untrustworthy. However, those who can't trust their own mother find it
normal to distrust someone until that someone proves they can be trusted.
I'm sure Jesus and Mother Teresa could live up to that trust challenge.
Most of us drop out and stop trying when we are continually distrusted
and put in the position of having to prove ourselves.

◇◇◇

Trust is learned around the age of two.
Therefore, if you can't trust your own mother, you most
likely learn that you can't trust anyone.
If you grow up believing that you can't trust anyone,
everyone you meet has to earn your trust.
Jesus and Mother Teresa are impeccable enough to earn
trust.
The rest of us . . . .

◇◇◇

Friendships frequently form from the connection of enjoying similar
things. Virginia *enjoys almost nothing*, again making it difficult for her
to form relationships. Friends meet for lunch or coffee. Virginia can't do
any of these social niceties, either. There is little fertile ground for Virginia to develop friendships.

Virginia *believes in a strict, punitive God.* I include this as a sign of
her anxiety, because in addition to never being able to please her mother
and never being able to please herself, Virginia also has been unable to
please her God. She believes the Crohn's is a punishment. She had lived
the high life as a professional athlete, had started to feel powerful and
capable, had been proud of her skills. She had been interviewed, written
about, sought after, cheered. Her religious background made her conclude that God had not liked her success. So, God had stripped her of that
life and given her the disease to humble her. Then He had seen to it that
she had been forced to come back home and work on making peace with

her mother. "This," she explains, "is why I said I had to fix my relationship with my mother. That's my top priority."

Her Steps

Virginia came to therapy once a week for two years. This gave us a great foundation.

She **took notes on her conversations with her mother**, so we could talk about the content and the process. The first thing we noticed was that the conversations were about her mother, and not often about Virginia. After Virginia said, "Hello," her mother launched into what Virginia's father had done or not done, what Virginia's sister-in-law had said or not said, especially regarding the grandchild, what the employees at the dry-cleaners had done or not done, and what Virginia, herself, had done, not done, said, or not said.

Interestingly, Virginia frequently erred by not reading her mother's mind. For example, "You didn't come home for lunch today and I had bought us two big seafood salads from that expensive new deli and I had to throw yours out. Since you weren't here, I wasn't hungry for mine. I don't know why I got such a thoughtless daughter." And all this over a plan her mother had hoped for, but neglected to mention to Virginia. I asked Virginia what her mother would say if she explained that she hadn't been invited for lunch. Virginia didn't even pause: "Oh, so now you're going to hold it against me that I thought you might be respectful enough to drop in and surprise me!" We decided perhaps Virginia should **forgive herself for her lack of mindreading skill**.

Virginia's mother called her between six and ten times a day. I suggested to Virginia that she **stop answering the phone**. I further suggested she **call her mother once a day** to begin with, less frequently later, and say some version of "I'm on my way to a meeting, mom, so I just called to see if there was anything you needed."

When the complaint came, which it would, that her mother could never get a hold of her, Virginia was to say, "**Leave** me **a message** on my phone. My message time is 60 seconds. I'll call you back when I can." She was to **call back** in whatever time frame was reasonable for the request. She was not to return the call at all if it was gossip or drama.

We agreed she should **not get hooked** by, "I wondered what you thought I should do?" What this meant in Virginia's mother's language was, *you tell me what you think I should do and then I will automatically and consistently shoot your idea down and do something else. I'm just* *setting you up for target practice.* When that question or any version of it was asked, Virginia and I decided she'd say some version of *I don't know, mom. But you're a clever woman and you'll figure it out.* Or, as they say in AA (Alcoholic's Anonymous): Just do the next right thing.

JUST DO THE NEXT RIGHT THING!
–AA

As is so often the case with a mother like Virginia's, Virginia's mother does not act out in the presence of people she considers to be powerful. Virginia's husband was considered by Virginia's mother to be a person of power. Consequently, **Virginia was only going to see her mother face-to-face when Russ could go with her.** I asked Virginia what Russ had thought of our plan. She laughed. She said he stood up, flexed his muscles for her, and said, "I'll protect you!"

It took a couple months of **continual and consistent boundary-setting**, but Virginia's mother started accepting and abiding by the boundaries. A good boundary doesn't leave much wiggle-room. And it's much harder to "hook-in" someone on a 60 second message than it is to wear them down in a 15 minute monologue. What always amazes people who are willing to try to set boundaries is that boundaries work.

Boundaries work.
That's why people use them!

The next most compelling source of stress in Virginia's life was her job. She was the office manager for a non-profit. She had worked her way up from two other jobs in the office. Her boss was relentless with her, and she yearned for her previous job. The salary had been lower, but so had the stress level. She had worked hard to earn this job as manager, and she hated to quit.

We spent a couple sessions trying to figure out ways Virginia could **reduce the stress at work** and get the boss off her back. We made lists and charts and used mnemonic devices to help Virginia work more efficiently and effectively.

Then one week, as we were talking about trying new things, I told her about my weekly adventure to an ethnic food store and how much fun I was having finding recipes on line and then tromping into a market where I didn't speak the language and showing the clerk the recipe or asking for something I was sure I was mispronouncing. I had found without exception that these endeavors left me and the clerk happy because we had these sweet, successful interactions. Virginia thought these forays were brave of me. I told her one of my mottos was, "If all I have to lose is my pride, I will not let that stop me from doing something."

She was all smiles when she came in for the next session. The woman who had taken Virginia's old job had resigned. As soon as Virginia heard this, she thought of my *Don't let your pride stop you* motto. She asked for and received her old job back. She said she felt like a paralyzing weight had been lifted from her. **She swallowed her pride, quit her more prestigious job and returned to a job that was virtually stress-free.**

◇◇

As a general rule for living:
Reduce stress. Reduce stress. Reduce stress.
Just remember what happens
to a balloon that's blown too tight.

◇◇

Virginia **cultivated some friendships at church**. These friendships were based on Bible Study and service projects, not lunches or coffees or drinks. These friendships seemed doable to Virginia. Perhaps, because they originated in a church setting, they seemed safe and meaningful and valuable to her.

She also **started cultivating some land in her backyard and she planted a garden**. She was astonished at the joy she found in getting her hands dirty. She is learning to tend to herself in some mysterious way as she learns to plant. All summer long she brings me fresh herbs. She has something of herself to share.

Virginia has also started living in her entire home. She told me early in our work that the only place in the house where she felt safe was in her bed. Not in the bathroom? She hates the bathroom. The bathroom represents humiliation to her. The kitchen? The living room? No, it turns out that she rarely sat down in her house, and if she did, it was only for a few minutes.

I asked her to tell me about her house and she described a window in the dining room that looked out over the backyard and the garden. The dining room, it turns out, was a big, empty room. I asked her if she could bring a chair and a table of some sort to that window, and if she might enjoy doing her daily devotions there. She experimented and found a rocking chair and a small end table to place in front of the window, and she now has **a second safe place to sit in her home**. Then I asked her about other furniture. It turns out they had none. Russ wanted to buy a sofa, but they hadn't. So, they did. And that led to painting the living room and decorating with some pillows and plants. She said Russ was so happy. They no longer watched television from the floor and they had begun to enjoy their home.

Feelings of unworthiness show up in surprising ways. Virginia felt unworthy of living in and bonding with her own home. She had lived there for three years as an unwelcome visitor. Just as she felt disconnected from her own body, she, too, felt disconnected from her own home. Virginia had been unable to make her living space warm or inviting, even for just her and her husband.

Then, about four years into our work, I got a phone message cancelling our next appointment. Her mother had died.

Since her boundary-setting, Virginia and her mother had developed a much more congenial relationship. Virginia found she actually wanted to call her mother sometimes, and Russ had participated in everything with them for long enough that they had found some lighter, less stressful ways of being together. And now her mother had died. I expected anger and resentment and overwhelming guilt.

What came to the next appointment was a relaxed, calm Virginia. "I'm free," she said. "She's free. And now I'm free, too." She felt a profound **sense of relief** that her unhappy, insatiable, highly critical mother was at peace. Virginia's mother died, and Virginia **released herself from the shackles of being a good daughter**, even though winning her mother's approval had always been impossible. She no longer had to try and fail. She was free. She was free in a way in which she had never felt free in her entire life.

During our years of therapy **Virginia's beliefs about God altered**. She was very good at quoting Bible verses to prove her points, mostly from the Old Testament. But she believed in Jesus, and so I would challenge her to think that perhaps Jesus came with new teachings.

As good as she was about quoting chapter and verse, I was no slacker myself. And so we'd honestly try to puzzle out together what God wanted us to know and believe. Most therapists would never bring up religious beliefs or argue them with clients. I'm the same way. But most of us will talk about religion or spirituality when the client begins the discussion.

That's no different than talking about anything else with which the client is struggling.

Virginia's religious beliefs were strongly influenced by her mother's Catholicism, which was a version that called for earning what you got from God through sacrifice and sanctity. Virginia and I spent a lot of time unraveling her theology and separating the wheat from her mother's chaff.

◇◇◇

Have you heard the theory that our ability to conceptualize God is based on our experiences with our parents? If we have loving parents, we conceptualize a loving God. If we have critical, judgmental parents, we conceptualize a critical, judgmental God. If we cannot trust our parents to protect us, we wonder if we can trust our God to protect us. As with every other theory I've ever heard, there are sure to be exceptions. But in my experience . . . this is more true than not.

◇◇◇

Virginia came to see her mother not solely as a villain, but also as a victim. Her mother was a woman of low self-esteem, high anxiety, and a multitude of mental health issues. Show me a critical adult, and in time, with enough information, we'll be able to see how wounded that person was as a child. Happy children who are loved, nurtured and protected, simply do not grow up to be demanding, critical adults.

Seeing her mother in this new, less judgmental way helped Virginia to judge herself less harshly, too. She came to believe that God might not be such a harsh judge either.

Virginia started working on empowering herself. We talked about power being control over ourselves and control being power over others. Her mother had very little personal power, and so she needed to control others. Remember the stream of dry cleaning workers Virginia's mom fired for minor infractions? How does one establish one's control? And what is the difference between control and power? And what a wonderfully Christian concept empowerment seemed to Virginia. Virginia came to believe that her own power came from **trusting God and knowing that God wanted only good for her.**

I reminded her that Jesus said, "I have come to bring you life abundant." That means, I added teasingly, life with a garden and a sofa and pretty painted walls and a stress-free job and unlimited safe places in your own home.

My Story

One of the funniest things that ever happened to me in therapy happened one night with Virginia.

We used relaxation tapes from the very first session. When we were down to our last 15 minutes of the session, she'd put her feet up and close her eyes and I'd put on soft music and start reading one of the relaxation scripts from Joan Boreschenko's Invisible Warriors. In this book the author presents different texts for different issues, including trauma, body image, anxiety, chemical dependency and much, much more.

Virginia and I had been talking that night about the difficulty she had been having sleeping. I opened the Invisible Hereos book, and noticed a script for help with sleeping. I was excited. "Shall we try it?" I asked. She looked doubtful but said, sure, why not. One of the other scripts was a favorite of hers, and I think she had her heart set on that one, but she was willing to see what a new script might bring.

We started, Virginia with her feet hanging over the edge of the love seat, and me, concentrating on the new words and putting my heart into what they were saying. When I finished the script, I looked at her for the first time. She was sound asleep, breathing deeply and evenly. I thought maybe she was joking with me. Nope. She was asleep. I had read the entire script and the music was still playing softly in the background. I waited a few minutes.

It was 7:40. Our session was to have ended at 7:30. Luckily, she was my last client of the day. I had just spent 20 minutes trying to help her relax so she could go to sleep. That was supposed to have been later. After she got home. After I got home, too.

Well, I surely wasn't going to wake her up. I put the book down and put my feet up on the coffee table and closed my eyes.

At 8 o'clock she said, "You stopped talking!" I opened my eyes. She was still stretched out on the sofa with her eyes shut.

We agreed that the script for falling asleep worked really well. Note to self: no using this in a car.

Virginia is a delightful client and a woman in transition. She is learning to live, freely and joyfully. She has taught me a lot, of course. All my clients have.

I would say her anxiety has diminished from 80% to perhaps 30%. Now that her God is a nicer God, everyone around her seems to be nicer and kinder, as well.

She is presently working on a relationship with her dad, and she has gone part time at the non-profit in order to help her dad with the dry cleaning business. He hasn't had a vacation in 40 years. Virginia wants to make that happen.

Interestingly, Virginia has put signs up in all the stores saying things like, "We are a team!" and "We can do anything!" and "Let's work together to succeed!" She is cultivating relationships and trusting the hired help to work together for the common good.

She continues to do the next right thing. I'm so proud of her. But I'm going to have to start devising other things for her to work on. Surely her therapy can't come to an end? I'm not ready to release my fresh herb supplier. (Only kidding. I can buy a bag of almost any herb I want at the Asian market just down the street! For a dollar!)

GREGORY

His Story

When I first met Greg and Betty they had three teenagers. That alone, even if everything else in their lives was going well, qualified them for therapy in my book.

Don't forget the old adage: You don't have to be sick to get better.

Betty was one of those people who looked perfect. She was a golfer, and she frequently wore clothes that made you think she was a golfer. She and Gregory had a business together. They managed a golf course. This was a private course with 27 holes, a pro shop, a bar and a restaurant. She did all the accounting and money management. He did everything else.

Gregory was a bartender, a chef, a maitre d', a salesman in the pro shop, a championship golfer and a schmoozer extraordinaire. He could delegate, and he did, any or all of his jobs. But he could also do each of his jobs very well all by himself. He had a second in command for each position, but he was a hands-on boss. He saw it as his responsibility to run the business in good economic times and in bad. He needed to get leagues up and running and get wedding receptions booked in the club house. He needed to be constantly changing the menu so as to keep things new and fresh. And he needed to keep his golf game good, but not too good. He had to give guys a run for their money, but not be so predictably good that he could always win.

Gregory was a high school athlete. Baseball was his game then. He came to golf later and learned the sport at the very course he now managed. That's where he met Betty. She worked in the pro shop and the restaurant. Her father owned the course.

Gregory grew up in a small town and was a small town hero. He barely slid by in school, but that didn't matter for the young man who helped bring home the state trophies.

His parents rarely came to his sporting events, and when they did, his father always found something to criticize. His mom thought he walked on water, but his mom never went up against his dad on anything. So his dad would list his faults and mistakes, and his mom would walk away, distracted. Later he'd discover she'd made his favorite snickerdoodle cookies or washed his uniforms. Whenever Gregory and his mom were alone, she made sure he knew she thought he was the best thing since sliced bread. "I was my mom's favorite," he'd acknowledge. His mom now had Alzheimer's and was in a nursing home. His dad lived by him-self in the house in which they'd raised their family.

Gregory's two younger brothers had both moved away. One, career Air Force, was in Texas and rarely got home. The other, a high school teacher and coach, lived a few hours away. Both were married. Grego-ry thought both were happily married. They had a couple of kids each. Gregory was not involved with their lives. "This is all I care about," Gregory said, indicating Betty. "Betty and the kids are my family."

Betty was the baby in her family. Her two older brothers were super stars. One was an attorney and one a C.P.A. They shared an office build-ing. They were, in Betty's opinion, allowed to do anything they wanted while growing up. They were males. Betty and her mother had been best friends for Betty's whole life. Her father kept her under his watchful eye, and she was very well protected. She had no freedom as a child or teen and seemed almost proud of it. She had always been and still was "a very good girl." She announced to me, taunting Greg: "My father would kill Gregory if he knew."

"She thinks I had an affair," Gregory said quickly and defensive-ly. Betty hooted and made derisive noises. Gregory rolled his eyes. I groaned. I was apparently being set up to be the judge and jury. It was going to be up to me to rule on whether Gregory's behavior, whatever it turned out to be, constituted "an affair."

"What would you call it?" Betty hammered me. "I've got the cell phone records. And then five weeks ago he disappears overnight while he's at a golf tournament which just happens to be in the town where she lives." Betty started crying. "I'll never get over it," she sobbed.

"I explained to her over and over what happened with the dead cell phone and the medicine I took for a headache. I didn't hear the damn room phone."

"That is so lame," Betty said. "Who in their right mind would believe that? And besides, there's the porn, and I hate it. I've turned my back this whole time and this is the thanks I get. My dad would kill you. He'd pay for my divorce and you'd be out of a job and a family. Poof. Your whole life goes up in smoke. You are such an asshole."

And so it went. Explanations. Threats. I back-tracked to see what "the porn" meant. Apparently Gregory liked to spend his free time on the computer looking at pornography. Every time Betty found a site on the computer, she'd block it. Every time she blocked a site, he found a new one. More explanations, more threats.

"What attracted you to each other?" I asked, trying to get us back on some solid ground. Gregory, predictably, told me how beautiful Betty was and is. Betty, predictably, coming from her family of high achievers, cited his ambition and his "charm."

I asked Gregory about money. He pointed at Betty and told me she handled it. But I wondered if you worried about it, I persisted. He told me anyone would worry about money in this economy. No one needed to join a golf club or play golf or have drinks in a bar or go to a restaurant or buy things in a pro shop. Their whole business was a luxury that people didn't splurge on in rough financial times.

I found out a few more interesting things. They had five cars. Each of the three children, the youngest 16, had his or her own car. Betty and her mom loved to shop. Every Wednesday they went out to lunch and went shopping. Gregory paid for his mother's Alzheimer's care. And Gregory and Betty smoked pot every night before bed. In the summer, they sat out on the patio in the evening to smoke. In the winter, they went for a ride every night. All these things added up to a strong need for some serious money.

Betty chimed in with yet another complaint. She was the disciplinarian. Gregory

was the kids' friend. She actually had four kids. No one listened to her. No one respected

her. No one did anything around the house. Oh, and no one loved her. Especially not

Gregory. "I do love you, Betty. You're beautiful. You're a wonderful wife. You're a great mom. I tell you all the time how much I love you." He sounded exasperated.

I asked if I might see Gregory alone for a few sessions. Betty was very much in favor of the idea, since she thought this absolved her from any responsibility for the mess they were in and put the blame squarely on Greg's shoulders. He acquiesced. He could hardly appear to be intimidated by a mental health person, and a woman at that.

His Signs

Affairs. It turned out that Gregory had actually had four affairs in their 26 year marriage. Betty only found out about the most recent one.

Insomnia. Gregory did not sleep. This was his explanation for the pornography obsession. Who else is up between 3 a.m. and 5 a.m. waiting for you with baited breath and husky whispers? Perhaps because of his insomnia, and perhaps for other reasons, Gregory had a *pornography addiction.*

Emasculation. Gregory worked for Betty's dad and served at the whim of Betty's dad. He had no shared in the business, no portion of the profits from the business, but did have Betty's constant threats of "My dad will kill you if" . . . this or that. He was constantly mindful of the fact that his wife co-signed his paychecks with his father-in-law.

Gregory was *worried sick about money.* Gregory was a nice guy, not a brilliant entrepreneur. He was everybody's best friend, and no one was afraid of him. His apprentice chef had a cocaine addiction and his fellow bartender, a young, single mom, skimmed money from the cash drawer.

Gregory did love Betty, but he wanted some praise and got only Betty's sharp tongue and disapproval. He didn't bring in enough business, he didn't come up with enough new ideas, and he didn't discipline or gain the respect of his employees or his children. "He's everyone's buddy," Betty complained. Everyone likes him. Everyone tells him their secrets. Betty sounded jealous. Perhaps Betty was jealous. Maybe that was why Betty withheld her praise and validation. But, for whatever reasons, Betty made it very clear that *Gregory simply could not measure up to her standards.*

The pot put him to sleep at night, but *his anxiety woke him in the middle of each and every night.* When I suggested to Gregory that he suffered from anxiety, he thought it was the craziest idea anyone had ever had. "I'm always in trouble for being too laid back," he argued. "Do you feel laid back at 3 a.m.?" I asked.

Gregory felt like *he lived in a house of cards.* Every time he handled one crisis, two new crises appeared. Betty was constantly complaining about their home, which she said "was falling down around them." Gregory simply *could not dance fast enough.* And yet his livelihood depended on him portraying himself as a care-free, friendly guy. *Gregory felt like a fraud.*

His Steps

For all the wrong reasons, Gregory **came into therapy**. This, in and of itself, might have continued to lower his self-esteem if he had met judgment and criticism anddisgust. Instead, he found therapy to be a safe place. In therapy he found understandinginstead of condemnation.

Actually, it was perfectly understandable why Gregory looked to other women for attention and affection. He wanted to feel again with someone what he had felt growing up: someone, like his mother in the past, who found him to be absolutely remarkable in the present. Gregory, with only a high school diploma and his personality and his ambition, was supporting himself, a wife, three children, a mother in an Alzheimer's facility, and, at least partially, his parents-in-law. And, he was doing it in quite a top-notch fashion. Under his management, the club brought in over $500,000 a year. And this was in Ohio, where we had at best a six month golf season.

Greg had expanded the services of the club to include all kinds of parties and celebrations. He devised the menus. The club was written up in a local magazine. Then, on top of that, he supported his kids in their endeavors and activities – sports, dance, academics. In addition to paying for his mother's care, he visited her at least twice a week. I would have wondered when this guy slept, if I hadn't already known that he didn't.

So, I simply **reflected back to him the scope of what he was accomplishing**. We talked about his insatiable craving for validation, and I explained to him that he had chosen to marry his father, the critic, not his mother, the nurturer. As I mentioned earlier, Harville Hendrix, author of Getting the Love You Want, believes we marry the negative aspects of our parents, or the parent with whom we've had the more difficult relationship. If our dad, like Gregory's, was critical, we are drawn to someone equally critical for our marriage partner. It seems illogical and counter-intuitive, but Hendrix's explanation is that we are unconsciously driven to re-write history. This time, by the sheer force of our love, we are going to silence those critics and make them love and accept us.

The next step, after we realize that we have foisted upon our spouse the impossible burden of making up for the inadequacies of our childhood, is that we **accept responsibility for ourselves.** We alone can heal our wounded inner child. We alone can learn to validate and affirm ourselves. As long as we depend on others for our self-esteem, we keep ourselves dependent, vulnerable and victimized. When we accept responsibility for our own self-awareness and self-affirmation, we become independent adults.

◇◇

As long as we depend on others
for our self-affirmation and self-worth,
we are dependent victims.
When we learn to affirm and reassure ourselves,
we find our own self-worth and claim it.
Then we become healthy, mature, independent adults.
When we no longer need praise, we can enjoy it when it
comes.

◇◇

Gregory and Betty took the Myers/Briggs Personality Invento-ry. (For a detailed explanation of the Myers/Briggs, see the Her Steps section of Paula's Case Study earlier in this book.) The results were that Gregory was an ENFP. Betty was an ISTJ. Exact opposites. We spent a very helpful session on these results. Once a couple sees and understands their similarities and differences, they can no longer blame each other for pushing their buttons and harassing them.

Gregory was an extrovert (E) and Betty was an introvert (I). He need-ed people and needed to be interacting with people. She needed a lot of time alone in her own head.

Look how people-intensive his hands-on managerial position was, and look how solitary her financial work was. Their jobs suited their per-sonalities. But Gregory could no longer harass Betty for not wanting to stay out late with him, and Betty could no longer harass him for always wanting people around. Yup, he always did need people around. That's how an extravert gets his energy. People re-charge him. And she did, in-deed, need quiet nights at home. She was an introvert, and people drained her energy.

Gregory was intuitive (N) and Betty sensing (S). Once again, look at their occupations. Food, for example, is not something that is right or wrong. People who are intuitive live in the gray, not in the black and white. Gregory worked on enhancing and improving his menus, the golf greens, the ambiance of the restaurant. A baked potato isn't "wrong" if it's served closed; it's just more appetizing if slit open with some sour cream and herbs on top. Betty, on the other hand, a sensing person, dealt with the black and white of numbers. And one of the things that made Betty so critical was that she didn't see a messy living room as something that could be enhanced by some picking up and putting away. She saw it as wrong. Bad. The messy living room was a personal statement of disrespect to her.

Gregory was a feeler (F) who made decisions in his heart and valued relationships more than logic. This was one reason Betty thought he was too friendly with their children. His relationship with each of them was more important to him than whether the grass got mowed on Monday, as he had asked, or not until Friday. Betty made decisions in her head. She was a thinker (T). If the grass needed to be mowed on Monday, then that was the day it should happen. That was only right and logical. So she worked to make it happen at whatever cost to her offspring's good will.

And, then, lastly, Gregory was a perceiver (P). His great strengths were making it up as he went along, shooting from the hip and going with the flow. Run out of green beans, serve asparagus. Run out of tomatoes, put a beet slice on the top of that salad. Betty is judging (J), which is not an accurate word to describe this characteristic. "Js" are planners and organizers. Betty would have planned ahead and had enough beans and tomatoes. No substitutions in her world. She wanted the clubhouse and her own home to run like a tight ship. When she played golf, the ball stayed on the fairway. When Gregory played, his shots were all over the place, from the sand traps to the rough. He made some amazing shots. Betty made predictable shots – nothing too bad, nothing too risky.

Now, **opposites attract**. And to have totally different talents means that the whole gamut is covered. But, a pre-requisite to this healthy thinking is the understanding that each of us comes into the world wired. Our life experiences either minimize or maximize the pre-existing wiring. Sounds a lot like nature and nurture, doesn't it?

Gregory worked on **finding his affirmation and validation within himself**. This allowed him a whole new set of responses to Betty's criticism. Instead of just folding when she demanded to know why they ran out of tomatoes, which showed a lack of planning which was unacceptable in her world view, Gregory could answer, "So I could try something new. It gave me a chance to be creative."

Gregory also came to **see some of Betty's rigidity as fear**. She was afraid not to plan every single detail for fear something would go wrong, and she wouldn't be able to think of some new, creative solution. We talked about the opportunity for Gregory to teach Betty to relax and to help her learn to make things up as they went along. Maybe the grass really was a little long by Friday, but Tuesday or Wednesday would suffice. And if they ran out of steaks, Gregory could create a beautiful shrimp special and actually save a little money. If one of the foursomes was slow and things got clogged up on the back nine, the beverage cart was sure to make some extra sales.

Gregory was willing to **examine his use of pornography**, which he said was not for masturbation. When asked when he was truly able to turn his mind off and relax, he said when he was watching porn. He agreed there might be other things he could watch or games he could play on the computer which might also be relaxing, but, he insisted, he just liked the porn. I pointed out that when we like something that's causing a relation- ship problem, we might want to examine *why* we like it and if we like it *that much.* Betty never had any problems with the porn until she found out about the affair. Perhaps he'd have to "man up" and take a voluntary hiatus. How important was Betty's happiness to him?

Gregory and Betty **took a vacation**. It had been more than 15 years since they had gone away alone together. They threatened the kids con- cerning good behavior, alerted the neighbors that they were leaving with- out the children and headed off in the car. Betty, the planner, had made reservations at a resort in a neighboring state. They only lasted three days, but it was a start. They both reported they had a great time, and at the next session they laughed like guilty teenagers when I asked them what they had done on vacation. I never did get a direct answer, but the giggling was pretty revealing.

My Story

It's always interesting as a therapist to see what brings people into therapy, what keeps them in therapy and what the actual therapeutic is- sues turn out to be.

As a marriage and family therapist, my inclination is to probe under- neath whatever appears and see what the present stuff is built on. Family roles and rules and responses were clearly very important in this case, so digging paid off here.

Gregory had a critical father and a *secretly* overindulgent mother. Secretly? Interesting that Gregory grew up to crave the *secret* affirmation and the adoration from affairs. He married his critical father. He was the oldest child, and so he needed accomplishment and achievement, while under fairly constant critical attack with only his mother's sporadic, *se- cret* affirmation.

Betty was the baby in a family of successful people. She grew up protected from the realities of the world and was spoiled and fawned over. She was willing to work hard, and she did. Her family had a strong work ethic. She simply expected something in return. She needed to be "the darling," "the baby," the one for whom things are planned and prepared and sanitized.

As is so often the case in marriages, both Gregory and Betty were keenly aware of what they needed and weren't getting from each other. Our work in therapy was to take that responsibility off each other's shoulders and begin to assume individual responsibility for what each needed.

Greg and Betty didn't last very long in therapy. I think and hope that we got some pressure off each of them and off of their relationship. I think they left with increased awareness of what they were doing unconsciously and how to become more accountable and transparent.

Sometimes, as with this couple, a therapist just gets a "slice of life" to observe and participate in. I got just that with Gregory and Betty. It's like reading only the ninth and tenth chapters of an eighteen chapter book. Makes you wonder about the rest of the story.

I want to comment, too, for those of you who are waiting in attack mode, about Gregory and Betty's pot use. When clients are under 21, that is, they are not legally adults, my comments are swift and black and white. It's illegal. You cannot use drugs, you cannot drink, etc., etc. When adult clients talk about drug use, each therapist must react in a way that is true and coherent for her.

The concern I expressed immediately to Gregory and Betty was the influence and example they were setting for their children. They told me the kids had no idea they smoked pot. I found that ludicrous, and I'm sure the expression on my face revealed that. As far as they knew, the kids did not smoke pot. In my very small and non-representative observations, parents who smoke, either cigarettes or pot, usually have children who do the same.

As therapists and counselors, we are legally bound to report clients who talk about suicide, homicide or clients whom we know or believe to be abusing a child. Those are, succinctly, our legal guidelines.

Some therapists are taught and work under the guidelines that they will not do therapy with someone who is abusing drugs or alcohol. Abusing is, of course, the tricky word. Who is to say what constitutes abuse? Whose definition and whose judgment do we follow?

Other therapists are taught to work with the clients who appear before them and to work with them in the condition in which they appear.

These therapists take the client where he or she is and try to work from there to optimize health.

Who knows what is right and what is wrong? Actually, a lot of people believe they do. I am not one of those people. I do remember question #1 on our college Human Sexuality final exam: what constitutes sexually appropriate behavior between adults. The answer: anything agreed upon by the two consenting adults. Some couples, for instance, use pornography in their sex lives. In this case, Betty wanted no part of it, and after finding out about his affair, wanted Gregory to cease and desist, too. On the other hand, for the past 15 years, they had ended every day with marijuana. Marijuana is illegal. Just one of the many reasons why all the names and details in each of the case studies presented here are fictionalized. Why, come to think of it, I might even have made up the part about the marijuana.

SUSAN

Her Story

(Portions of this story are from journal entries written during what I assumed was an anxiety attack.)

I sat on an airplane seat, the middle of three, even though I had carefully chosen an aisle seat, and I felt my heart pounding. I had no energy to fuss about anything, least of all about where I was sitting. My heart was banging against the skin of my chest. It should have shown, like when you see an unborn baby rolling over and kicking his or her mommy's tummy.

The heat started inside me, and almost immediately I broke out into a sweat. I adjusted the air overhead, hoping for some relief.

Heartburn forced itself into my awareness. And then nausea. I wondered if I should look in the pocket in front of me for a bag.

We were sitting on the runway. I was headed to a totally non-stressful week away. And now that all the responsibilities were handled, the arrangements made, the bills paid, the family all healthy and happy, as happy as possible after our third family funeral in three months, and everyone was headed back to where they belonged, now . . . Now, I was having an anxiety attack.

I had spent four months last spring easing myself off Celexa, an anti-depressant I had been on for about six years. It is frequently prescribed for those with some anxiety as well as depression because it contains a good anti-anxiety component along with a Selective Serotonin Reuptake Inhibitor. As an SSRI, it keeps serotonin, the feel-good chemical, in the brain. Stress pushes serotonin out of the brain and into the body. We need it in our brains on a daily basis and in our bodies only in case of an emergency. When people get overly stressed, their emergency response system goes awry and stays constantly in gear. An SSRI fixes the problem. And I had been on such an SSRI, worked hard to get off one, and was now taking only Theanine, the over-the-counter herbal supplement we talked about in Amanda's case study. As you may remember, it helped her kick her bulimia.

This particular anxiety episode of mine had started the day before the airplane adventure while I was seeing a few last clients before I left on vacation. One young man in particular was talking about how his anxiety had worsened. Now, not only could he not drive over bridges, but he couldn't ride on escalators or be a passenger in cars. I suggested he was having trouble with small spaces. He shook his head from side to side. "Elevators are fine."

"Damn anxiety," I remember saying. "It comes when it wants, then stays for as long as it pleases."

And within the hour it was inside my chest. It wasn't inside my head. I wasn't thinking anxious thoughts. My thought were calm and focused. We had just made it through, as I said, a third family funeral, but now it was all over. We had done what we could, and more, and the out-of-town family was driving home even as the anxiety was driving itself into my chest.

Maybe that's it, I thought. Maybe I'm just worried about everyone getting back where they belong. When I hear that they're home, maybe this anxiety and tension and heaviness and shakiness will vanish. (Am I or am I not the same person who wrote repeatedly throughout this book that anxiety was not logical, it was a feeling, and it often did not have a present moment cause? I swear, when you're in the midst of things yourself, everything you know, or think you know, vanishes!)

So, I lectured myself. You spend your days talking to other people about anxiety, I told myself. You know better. Sometimes there is a logical or attributable accelerator, but the anxiety itself seems to sit and wait. Sometimes it comes because you're so sure it will, that it does. But most of the time, anxiety arrives like a stealth bomber.

My best guess is that anxiety acts like so many other health predispositions. Genetically, some of us have inherited The Anxiety Gene. Some people get The Depression Gene, The Cancer Gene, The Foolhardy Gene, The Math Gene, The Addictive Personality Gene, The Musical Gene, and so on. Some genetic predispositions are quite handy. Some make us quite hardy. Some are quite hampering. Some handicap us.

I've observed in clients that those who are "pleasers" often fall prey to Marital Anxiety. This is the anxiety which is triggered, if we have the anxiety gene, when we try to negotiate with, accommodate, and/or please another. In many cases, as in Mike's, in his earlier case study, this is particularly true when one is in relationship with someone who is insecure, or condescending, or critical or blaming. Being held responsible for things which are not our fault, or being expected to mind-read the needs and wants of another, can definitely be a building block for anxiety.

For one client this type of anxiety led to colitis. (Colitis is a digestive disease similar to Crohn's disease, which we talked about in Virginia's case study.) A few years after she developed colitis she divorced, and the colitis went away. (Many, many medical problems are begun, intensified and compounded by anxiety.) She told me that shortly after the divorce she had to change doctors. The new doctor corrected her when she said she had previously had colitis. "Colitis doesn't go away," the doctor insisted. My client insisted that her colitis did go away. Completely. "How?" the doctor demanded, as though my client knew some medical secret. "I got divorced," she confided. The doctor laughed out loud. Like my client, I don't find anything funny about divorce, but she admitted she was delighted to be divorced from the colitis.

After a divorce many of us have to face our fear of being alone in a house, our heartbreak at having become divorced, and/or our need to be a single parent. I would get shaky and sleepless, for example, but therapy and exercise seemed to limit the intensity of these problems. As I grew more confident as a single mom, and as it became apparent that the children and I would continue eating and having a roof over our heads, my anxiety dissipated and then disappeared.

Another very typical time for depression and anxiety to come flooding in is after a spouse deserts or abandons us, especially if, for whatever reasons, we don't see it coming. It's almost as if the anxiety and depression rush to fill the space the spouse or lover left vacant. For me, at 53, with my children grown, I was facing a second "failed marriage," as people like to call them. Please, I beg you, **do not** use that term.

This new development was entirely off the radar of my personal life script. As for my professional life script, I found myself a twice divorced marriage and family therapist. As one of my clients said just a month ago, "Why should we trust her to help us with our marriage? She's divorced." Interestingly, it was the first time in my 25 year career that anyone had suggested this.

In the twelve years since my second divorce, I've been plagued with anxiety. And I am surely not alone or different from many of you reading this book. Gradually, we accept the realities of who we are and what we are, as we build, many of us for the first time, a life of our own. Many of us have created a happy, safe, fulfilling life. I amaze myself with how independent I've become. I've learned to enjoy my own company. (Actually, I think I'm rather amusing!) And I hear clients tell me that they share these feelings. Left, and then left to our own devices, we do amazingly well. We often amaze ourselves!

So, we have healthy, happy purposeful, independent people with anxiety? Yes.

As I write this, I'm on day seven of what is undoubtedly the most pervasive, pernicious anxiety attack I've ever experienced. Anxiety is not logical. It comes when it pleases, stays as long as it wishes, and departs, sometimes, as mysteriously as it arrived.

◇◇◇

Anxiety is not logical.
Anxiety comes when it pleases.
Anxiety stays as long as it wishes.
Anxiety leaves when it chooses.
Anxiety is not logical.

◇◇◇

Her Signs

I am logically and rationally unaware of any reason why I would be tense or anxious right now. We have to start there to understand anxiety. *Why are you anxious?* or *What do you have to be anxious about?* are irrelevant questions.

While present anxiety may well have a slew of past causes, most decidedly the familial and genetic predisposition to anxiety, it rarely has an identifiable present cause or reason. What anxiety does have is a lot of signs. Everyone's sign are different, although the *shaky, tense, hyper, sleepless, unable-to-calm-down* signs seem to hit all of us who are anxious.

In addition, I had about a dozen of my own signs. My *heart wouldn't stop pounding.* Unlike my usual steady, distinct heartbeat, this anxious heartbeat was more of a drum roll. The beats of my heart seemed indistinguishable, and my heart seemed to beat continuously rather than in a punctuated rhythm.

I was *short of breath.* I had been increasingly active for the last six months and was rarely short of breath anymore. All of a sudden, starting that Saturday when I saw those last few clients before vacation, I couldn't seem to catch my breath. When my breathing would slow down, like when I started to fall asleep, or relax, all of a sudden I'd find it hard to breath, and I'd startle myself awake trying to get a good, deep breath.

Sleep was particularly awful. If I did fall asleep, I'd jerk myself awake, *hyperventilating. I couldn't get settled. I couldn't relax. I was constantly moving around, trying for a comfortable, easy position. Although it was cool in my bedroom, I often found myself sweating.*

My head and shoulders were tense and tight. My throat felt constricted. I wondered if I had a sinus infection, my head felt so heavy and thick. But I didn't have a sore throat or a runny nose or a cough.

I felt light-headed and found myself needing to concentrate so as not to faint.

I couldn't get comfortable. If I was lying down, I'd need to sit up. If I was sitting up, I'd feel like I needed to lie down and stretch out.

I was in no pain, but *I was truly miserable.*

Emotionally I was *tearful and felt like crying* over everything and anything. Telling a simple story or watching a dog rescue on television brought tears to my eyes.

I was *highly irritable.*

Okay. I'm going to stop there, because, as the saying goes, "that was all she (I) wrote" when I was in the midst of my trauma. For seven days I struggled with what I thought was anxiety. Actually, I landed in the hospital for the next six days. I was having trouble with my heart and was in atrial fibrillation, a medical condition where your heart gets stubbornly out of rhythm. Remember my description of my heart beat as a drum roll instead of a distinct, steady beat. Reading back over what I wrote at the end of that vacation I can now see all the clues. But, to give myself a little grace, let me tell you about my history of A-fib, as we regulars call it.

Six weeks after my mother died I was in the hospital for five days, admitted with a heartbeat of 198 beats per minute. Medicine alone would not get my heart slowed down or back in rhythm, and it had to be shocked back into submission. The cardiologist kept me on medicine for nine months and then he and I decided that it had been a fluke that my heart had gotten out of whack. I titrated slowly off the medication, stayed on the Celexa, and resumed life. About two years later I got sick at work one day with all those same symptoms. I was lightheaded, my heart was racing, and I was hyper, shaky and tense. Off to the hospital I went. This time there was nothing wrong with my heart. Since my heart was beating slowly and regularly, the diagnosis was anxiety.

Now, along comes episode #3, and having been embarrassed to have gone to the hospital with anxiety, I assumed this was anxiety again. And I launched into all the things I do for anxiety: breathing, exercise, writing. Actually, I think I'm lucky I didn't kill myself. The worse I felt, the more I exercised. Great move, eh? Get a heart that's already beating erratically and too quickly beating a little faster.

Well, I explain all this to make a point which I hope you will never forget. ***Anxiety does not last relentlessly for seven days***. But, there are a great many physical problems which mimic the symptoms of anxiety. A-fib, mitral valve prolapse and congestive heart failure might all feel like anxiety. Gastro-intestinal issues are usually the first place stress hits us, and colitis, Crohn's, IBS and other gastro-intestinal diseases all include anxiety-like symptoms. How could they not? Headaches, migraines, and tinnitus (ringing in the ears), are also illnesses that look like and feel like anxiety.

What I hope you'll remember is this: ***just because you have anxiety doesn't mean every time you get shaky or short of breath or start hyperventilating it is your anxiety***. Unfortunately, anxiety does not provide protection from other illnesses. When in doubt, I beg you, go to the doctor or the hospital. I have made up my mind that I don't care how many times I end up in the emergency room with anxiety and nothing wrong with my heart. I will never again put myself through the insanity of self-diagnosis and self-treatment.

Ben, a client I haven't previously talked about, is a talented observer of his own anxiety. He likens his anxiety to a volcano: lots of tremors, few eruptions. He says he has about 98 tremors for every two eruptions. And, he has observed, the eruptions last about fifteen minutes. Most of the time, he can calm himself down and plow his way through the tremors. When he can't, he knows that in about fifteen minutes and after a good sweat, it'll be over. He'll be tired for the rest of the day, he realizes. Other than that, he will have no lasting effects.

You might notice that Ben's description of fifteen minutes is significantly different from my endurance of seven days. Yes, I feel embarrassed and stupid, but I am forging on with my description because it is my hope that you will read this and be increasingly gentle with yourself. If I'm writing a book about it, and I can't always handle my own anxiety, or even consistently recognize it, maybe it's okay for you to blow it sometimes, too. Or, you may be deciding that I have no credibility for you because, as my clients observed, I'm not qualified to help with their marriage because I'm divorced. Perhaps I'm not qualified to help with your anxiety, either, since I have my own issues with anxiety. Or, perhaps I'm uniquely qualified.

Unfortunately, anxiety is not curable. It's containable, recognizable and treatable. The steps my various clients have taken have helped them with their anxiety problems, and whatever steps you choose for yourself will help you with your anxiety, as well.

I am now on three prescription medications for my heart. Knowing that I am taking medicine which will keep my blood thin, my heart beat slow and my heart beat regular and in rhythm are all helpful in reducing my anxiety. Keeping my anxiety down will help the medicine to do its job. This is the mind/body connection. What triggers our bodies triggers our minds, and vice versa.

If you suffer from anxiety, make sure you do everything in your power to remove any contributing physical issues. See your physician. If your physician "doesn't believe in anxiety" or treats you like a hypochondriac because you have anxiety, get a new doctor. Your health care provider, like your therapist, needs to believe in and accept your reality.

They say that as a writer, you need to create a rose garden that is so real that the reader can smell the roses. As a therapist or physician, you need to step into your client's/patient's rose garden and begin any work from that place. As counselors of either mental health or physical health, we can't expect our clients or patients to meet us in our garden. We go into theirs and get to know what makes them tick, mentally, emotionally, physically, spiritually, and then together we move on from there.

So, I close by imploring you to be kind to yourself. When people are saying good-bye to each other and say, "Take care," I hope those words will have new meaning for you as you focus more surely on caring for yourself. Virginia Satir, the mother of marriage and family therapy, believed that low self-esteem and poor self-care were the root of all the problems in marriages and families. It's up to each of us to make sure that low self-esteem and lousy self-care are not a legacy we pass on to our children. Remember, they don't hear a word we say, they only see what we do.

I know I've told this story before, but it bears repeating: A busy father was trying to entertain his son and get some work done at the same time. He tore from a magazine a page containing a map of the world. He tore the "world" into pieces and asked his son to put the map back together, thinking he had just bought himself a lot of time. Five minutes later the boy was finished. The startled dad asked him how he'd done it. The boy explained that there was a picture of a man on the other side of the page, and that when you get the person put back together, the world falls into place.

Possible Indicators of Anxiety

- Your mother was passive, aggressive, passive-aggressive, critical or mentally ill
- Your father was abusive, critical, absent or abandoning
- You suffered from any adverse childhood experiences
- You are rarely in the present moment
- You are busy predicting the future
- You are pre-occupied rehashing the past
- You have a chronic physical illness
- You have posttraumatic stress disorder, depression or another chronic mental health condition
- You are diagnosed with a life-threatening disease
- You get married, divorced or have an affair
- You suffer the loss of someone you love
- You suffer a trauma of any sort
- You are victimized in any way
- You lose your job for any reason
- You suffer financial changes, either positive or negative
- You work alone or from home, especially if this is a change
- You have a child
- You have a teenager
- You try to teach someone to drive

Symptoms of Anxiety
Partial List

(No complete list is possible since we are all so creative!)

- Tightness
- Rigidity
- Guardedness
- Tension
- Feeling vulnerable
- Feeling exposed
- Always expecting danger
- Shakiness, shivering or sweating
- A sense of dread
- Feeling like a "victim"
- Being docile or passive
- Being angry, aggressive or filled with rage
- Appearing humorless, lifeless, invisible: Mr. Cellophane from Chicago
- Feeling resigned or indifferent
- Being disengaged, having no trusted friends, having fractured family relationships
- Being hyper-alert
- Being a hoarder with money or possessions or spending recklessly
- Lack of concentration and focus
- Feeling dissatisfied and feeling like there is never enough, at least not for you

Notes to Therapists

A few last thoughts for my "fellow pilgrims" on this therapy trail: first an image for working with clients and secondly, of course, a friendly lecture on self-care.

First, the image for working with clients, whether the presenting issue is anxiety or something else: the puzzle.

Each life is a puzzle. The therapist enters each client's individual and idiosyncratic life at one specific moment in the on-going building of that puzzle. Usually, we enter a client's life at some moment of crisis. Our chances of having a client lay out for us, accurately and without prejudice, the important pieces of his or her life puzzle are zero. Therefore, it is up to us to build for the client and ourselves an accurate representation of who they are. We have to do this with a lot of pieces missing from the puzzle. We may even be working with pieces from a number of different puzzles.

Sorting out with clients which pieces belong to their own puzzle and which pieces came from the puzzles of the parents, their culture, and/or their religion is important. Is my Protestant work ethic simply a hanger-on from my parents and my church, or is it something I want to consciously welcome into the fabric of my life? Must I have all my work done before I can sit down, as my mother insisted? Must I pay a bill on the day it arrives, as my father role-modeled? What choices have I and can I make about the legacy I have carried unconsciously and the legacy I want to choose to carry as I become more self-aware?

Getting the disparate pieces of other people's life puzzles out of our puzzle box is a great start. To facilitate this, I often ask clients: Whose voice is that? Who can you hear saying that? Who taught you that? Is it valuable and true for you? And, so, we get the puzzle sorted. Then we're working with pieces from only one box, not multiple boxes. (Have your kids ever done that? Mixed puzzles together? Mine did. Makes me laugh now, but it wasn't very funny when it happened. It was overwhelming, just like it is in therapy. And it demanded a great deal of patience, just like it does in therapy.)

Now that we've got one box of puzzle pieces, we need to turn on the lights. In therapy, I think this means we need to gain whatever outside insight and guidance we can. I use the Myers/Briggs Personality Indicator and the Enneagram for this purpose. These tests help us answer questions about self-awareness and self-identity. What are your strengths? What is your personality like? Who were you born to be? Help with such insight will tell us which pieces of the puzzle are central and which pieces are simply ornamental trimmings. For example, I play the piano, but that really has little or nothing to do with who I am. I enjoy it, and I think my piano is a lovely piece of furniture, but I am not a musician at my core. It's a tangent, and any therapist who concentrated on that as an essential part of my being would confuse me.

On the other hand, cooking, for me, is a way to nurture myself and others. I would have to say that food, buying it, preparing it, serving it, is a core aspect of who I am. In fact, when I took the Enneagram and discovered I was a Two, I didn't have to explore to find out what my "wing" type was. One of the descriptors for a Three Wing was the word "hostess." Yup. That's me. I'm a Two with a Three Wing.

My cooking helped me figure out one of the Myers/Briggs categories, as well. The fourth dimension of the Myers/Briggs Personality Inventory is the distinguishing between being a "J" and a "P." "Js" like to do things in a coherent, organized fashion, starting with A and progressing to Z. That was my mom. She cooked the same things time after time and could tell you exactly how long to boil green beans (8 minutes, I think). She was a fabulous cook and I never knew her to burn anything or make anything that wasn't done perfectly. But she never made sauces, never experimented, never stepped outside the sure and certain box.

Meals are unpredictable in my house, the house of a "P." You're likely to get an apple sliced on top of your pork chop or dried cherries in your salad. But probably not twice. If I've done it once, I'm ready to try something new. I love experimenting. And when you experiment, you're going to have flops. I made some soup last week that was so uninspiring and uninspired, I threw it away yesterday. And I hate throwing food away, but that was exactly what this soup deserved. I'm a "P." We make it up as we go along. I know cooks who won't try a new recipe if they don't have all the ingredients. That would be a "J" characteristic. We "Ps" substitute. No sour cream? No problem. I'll use yogurt. The sauce sounds good, but I'm tired of chicken. No problem. Lets try it over shrimp.

These are strange details, perhaps, but they underscore the necessity of delineating the important pieces from the less important pieces. Getting to know oneself means getting comfortable with our foibles and uniqueness. And it is all okay. Every piece belongs. We are each created to be a valuable part of the eco-system of life. But we have to know who we are. That established, we can concentrate on and develop our own individual essence. We have to construct our own puzzle of life. A good therapist will help. A good therapist will help you turn on the lights and sort the pieces.

Now, about self-care. My friend and colleague, Marsha, believes that self-care has to do with open-heartedness. "When the energy flows out of your heart to someone else," she explained to me, "it comes back like a wave." She believes that, and she practices that. All summer long she spends her Sunday afternoons cooking for her neighbors. The combination of volunteering and nurturing feeds her soul. She maintains that summer cooking is one of her methods of self-care.

At least four of the 18 therapists I work with also find cooking to be a form of self-care. For me, choosing healthy foods and learning to prepare them is a challenge and a joy. Many of us will bring in recipes that we've tried that were particularly good, and when we find a new market for fresh produce or anything else, the excitement is strange to behold. We act as though we've discovered some cosmic secret.

All sorts of physical movement are, of course, wonderful self-care. One of the therapists with whom I work is a marathon runner. Another attends Tai Chi classes. At least five of us practice some form of yoga. Two walk the trails of the local parks. One is a belly-dancer. I dance in the kitchen with great abandon (but alone and unobserved).

We have a basket in the therapist's break room for books, and we are constantly bringing in books we've read and leaving with books others have read, as many of us find reading to be a fulfilling form of self-care. The variety of what we read runs the gamut from fiction to science fiction to self-help to psychology. A number of us read spirituality and, again, we delight in spreading the word of some new writer we've found.

Six of the therapists at work are artists. They make jewelry and pottery, paint and sketch, create collages and even plant terrariums. Which brings me to gardening, which is another vital form of self-care for a number of us. Nothing compares with planting a seed or sticking a limp little plant in the ground and watching it flourish and thrive. (Gardening bears some resemblance to therapy, doesn't it?)

I think all of us travel during the year, mostly, but not exclusively, within the United States. One therapist does mission work in Central America. A number of us have traveled abroad and a few of us have gotten to Asia. I joined a Mental Health mission team which went to China to facilitate sharing ideas about posttraumatic stress with our Chinese counterparts. Travel, whether for work, with our churches or professional groups, or for pleasure, refreshes the spirit and sends us home different people than the people who left on the trips.

Most of us have a very active spiritual life and credit that as our most vital form of self-care. Whether we read, attend services, meditate, volunteer, or have some other spiritual practice, I think we'd all agree that it is our belief in a Higher Power from which we derive our strength and our hope and our faith.

One of my clients had 17 epiphanies, or insights, this year. Number one on his list was: I will trust God in all things at all times. His other 16 epiphanies also had to do with loosening the tight control he had exercised over himself and his family. Perhaps it was going to be safe for him to relax, and, as another one of my clients likes to say, "Let God be in charge today."

Now I mention the man with the epiphanies because he and I spent so much time arguing God's character and intentions. He was sure God was punitive and didn't listen and had nothing good in store for him. Interestingly, nothing happened in his life to change this thinking. He didn't win the lottery or find a new love or experience any sort of external good fortune. He just chose to change the way he saw things and the way he lived. I mentioned that we had spent "so much time" on these issues. How much, you ask? Eighteen, yes, 18 years. Without my active spiritual life, I could not have hung in there waiting and hoping and praying for him to have a change of heart. We have to have something larger and smarter and wiser and more loving than we ourselves if we're to hang on and paddle the lifeboats with others.

One of the therapists at work told me she prays as she drives to work every day. "I can't do it, God. I give it all to You. I'll show up and handle the physical presence, and you do the work. Okay?" Then she relaxes into her day. She says, "I'm not even doing it. I'm just willing to lend myself."

I'm sorry to say most of us don't present that level of faith. We like to keep our fingers on the pulses and our hearts and minds engaged. But, I do think we'd all agree that the work of therapy is mysterious and awesome. Things happen that surely were not of our doing. This is not false humility. We all like to take some credit for being there and steering the boat. But what we encounter while on that boat . . . well, that is an ever-changing landscape and an often amazing experience. It's a puzzle. And sometimes some of the pieces fit, but always the puzzle itself is a work in progress.

So, take breaks, smile at children, get massages, and treat your mind and your body with kindness and compassion. And thank *you* for sharing this time with me.

Ideas from Bill Blocksom

Bill is a massage therapist extraordinaire.

"Possible ways to increase relaxation and decrease anxiety"

• Abdominal breathing. A few minutes a day can work wonders. It is especially useful when driving. The sound of the engine and the stress of traffic can cause us to become anxious. Conscious breathing into and through the abdomen will surely help. Breathing in and out through the nose, even when exercising, increases relaxation. Breathing through the mouth stimulates the sympathetic nervous system, the fight, flight or freeze mode.

• Try progressive relaxation using guided or self-hypnosis recordings.

• Tai-Chi, Qi Gong, Chi Gung and Yoga all espouse a gentle-with-yourself attitude.

• Soft music or gentle, natural sound recordings can be especially relaxing.

• Eat without distractions, like the television or the computer. Leave extra time at the beginning and the end of the day.

• Walk 30 minutes a day. That amount of time allows us to disengage from perseverating thoughts, and walking is good for our body, mind and spirit.

• Monitor your intake of caffeinated beverages, sugar and white flour.

• Use meditation techniques and practices first thing in the morning and last thing at night.

• Monitor your intake of news, current events, television and movies.

• Avoid negative people.

• Pray, as fits your belief system, morning and night.

• Before sleep review the day: what went well and what didn't. Then let it all go.

• Keep a gratitude journal. Write down up to 50 things for which you are grateful, but five or ten will do just fine. Re-read entries of the previous day each morning. That way you end and begin each day with a sense of gratitude.

• Connect with the earth, spirit guides, God, a teacher, other people and the larger community.

• Connect with friends or a friend over a cup of coffee or tea, or a glass of wine. It never fails that a few minutes with a friend can re-balance and sustain us.

There are a great many books and recordings which decrease tension and induce relaxation. You may want to try:

Richard Carlson's <u>Don't Sweat the Small Stuff</u>

Louise Hay's <u>You Can Heal Your Life</u>

Susan Jeffers' <u>Feel the Fear and Do It Anyway</u>

Gawain Shakti's <u>Creative Visualization</u>

These ideas come from my massage therapist: William S. Blocksom, LMT, Akron, OH
They are added here with his permission, but pale in comparison to the wisdom he imparts should you be fortunate enough to live near Akron and benefit from his expertise which includes massage and life.

About Susan Rau Stocker

Susan has spent her life communicating: listening, reading, writing, talking. A former college teacher, for the past twenty-five years she has been a marriage and family therapist in private practice. She has traveled extensively, read voraciously and written continuously–lesson plans, case notes, journals, grocery lists, stories, two published novels (formerly as Susan Ross, soon to be re-published under her own name), some journalism and a bit of scholarship. The Many Faces of Anxiety is her second "self-help book." The Many Faces of PTSD was her first. (You'll never guess the name of her third. Hint: Don't depress yourself trying to come up with it.)

The Many Faces of PTSD

This book tells the stories of twelve survivors of trauma. Each case study describes the survivor's trauma experience in gut-wrenching detail and then chronicles the interaction between the survivor and the therapist by tracing the stumbling, pitfall-ridden paths of both. The studies illuminate the signs and symptoms of posttraumatic stress disorder (PTSD) displayed by the survivor and the steps to recovery, both forward and backward. The final and most sagacious segment of each case study is the story of the therapist/author. One of the missing pieces in most narratives about the treatment of and recovery from PTSD is the perspective of the therapist, a living, breathing person with life experiences and challenges of his or her own. The Many Faces of PTSD fills in this missing piece with humility and humor.

Only Her Naked Courage

The working life of Sara Miller has been devoted to helping victims of heinous acts. As much as she knows about trauma and survival, nothing has or could have prepared her to become the victim herself. She is simply driving home from work one day, daydreaming about how happy she is, when she sees a woman stranded by the side of the road. She decides to stop and help. Life as she knows it ends with that decision. Sara, the social worker, who tirelessly leads victims back to sanity, is swamped in a nightmare more evil and depraved than any she has ever encountered. And she finds herself alone in her terror, left with one resource: Only Her Naked Courage.

Heart
(originally as Susan Ross)

It began one passionate evening and ended one bittersweet weekend. Ruth was leaving for the grandeur of Italy and the career of her dreams. Tom could never abandon his wife or the son who needed him so completely. So Ruth and Tom parted, perhaps never to touch again. But although they couldn't be together, they shared a love as enduring as the ocean that separated them. Theirs was a love more desperate than the tragedies they each had to face. Despite their knowledge that they could not change the course of their lives, neither Tom nor Ruth could forget the burning fire they ignited together. Something undeniable glowed deep and sure in each yearning Heart.